Benedetto Croce

ESSAYS ON
MARX AND RUSSIA

Selected and translated, with an introduction, by
ANGELO A. DE GENNARO
Loyola University of Los Angeles

FREDERICK UNGAR PUBLISHING CO.
NEW YORK

MILESTONES
OF THOUGHT
in the History of Ideas

Copyright © 1966 by
Frederick Ungar Publishing Co., Inc.

Printed in the United States of America

Library of Congress Catalog Card No. 66-17538

CONTENTS

CONTENTS

INTRODUCTION

Benedetto Croce was born in 1866 in Pescasseroli, a village of the mountainous Abruzzi, into a family of wealthy landowners. He was very precocious, exhibiting even in his high school years the great intellectual curiosity that was always one of his chief qualities. It is not unimportant, I think, to mention that he was always the first in his class and many times received scholastic honors. At seventeen, Croce and his family were caught in the earthquake of Casamicciola in which he lost his parents and his only sister. We sense in his writings that this experience left an unforgettable imprint on his life.

Between 1885 and 1886, he studied at the University of Rome under the Italian Marxian thinker, Antonio Labriola, who exercised a great influence on the young student. In 1886, without completing his formal studies, he returned to Naples. Here, left on his own, he devoted himself to the study of foreign languages and humanistic studies, among those Neapolitan history and the works of De Sanctis, Vico, Marx, Hegel, and others.

At the same time, he stimulated a great revival of philosophical studies in Italy with the founding of the famous periodical *La Critica* (1903) and with his collaboration with Giovanni Gentile on the Bari series of *Classici della filosofia*. To the latter, he contributed

the important works on Vico and Hegel: works in
which he portrays Vico as the discoverer of the true
concept of aesthetics and Hegel as the rediscoverer of
the principle of contradiction.

An immense influence has been exerted by Croce's
systematic works: *Estetica* (1902), *Logica* (1909), *Filosofia della pratica* (1909). The *Estetica* is the most important book and, despite some detractors, still remains a classic. Proceeding from Vico and De Sanctis,
Croce sets himself against the hedonistic, moralistic,
naturalistic aesthetics and expounds his famous principle of art as intuition-expression.

The publication of Croce's systematic works produced mixed results. Many were enthusiastic for the
new doctrines and became his fervent disciples. But
there were others within the academic community who
said, to Croce's chagrin, that he was nothing but a
blind follower of Hegel. For the remaining four decades, Croce was to vigorously engage in explaining his
doctrines and in defending himself against his detractors. The result was astounding: Croce became an
Italian institution and the dean of Italian scholars.

In the twenties, Croce became the outstanding adversary of fascism. This was because of his writings on
history, which were altogether too liberal for fascist
taste. The publication of his *History of Italy* in which
Francesco Crispi, the hero of fascism, was ridiculed
strengthened Mussolini's hostility for Croce. At all
events, he continued to extol the forbidden love for
liberty in his works.

Croce's last years were fruitful. Though he was in
his seventies, he was the minister without portfolio in
the governments of Badoglio and Bonomi, the founder

of the Italian Institute of Historical Studies, the re-
founder of the Liberal Party. Nor did his advanced age
interfere with his scholarly life: he continued to write
on history, literary criticism, politics, and philosophy
until his death in 1952, in Naples, at the age of 86.

Croce's thought is essentially idealistic: there is one
reality—the Spirit or the Absolute. We meet this quality at the beginning of his speculation, and it gives a
particular tone to all his writings on art, history, and
ethics. Art is seen as spirituality or individuality and
not as an objective reality. For Croce, as well as for
Kant, there is no beauty outside the spirit: beauty is
the projection of the spirit or mind. Thus Croce opens
an entirely new world: the difference between form
and content, the classification of the arts, translation,
the chasm between genius and taste, literary criticism,
language, and history of art are profoundly affected.
In regard to the problem of form and content, Croce
affirms that there is no difference between the two.
Good content or deep feeling always expresses itself
in good form. Poetic translation is declared an impossibility. Poetry is not water that one can pour from
one vase into another. Poetry is individuality, spirituality, uniqueness. Genius and taste are declared iden-
tical. The difference between the two only consists in
the diversity of circumstances: one is a productive activity; the other is a reproductive activity. Traditional
criticism is rejected. The critic must approach the
poet's world and must search for the poet's spirituality, the fundamental motif, and should not reduce
poetry to a complex of historical observations. Also
the critic must not show the superiority of one poet's
artistic world over that of another. If poetry is spirit-

uality, one poetical world cannot be compared with another. Language as a logical expression is discarded. Language is not a complex of ideas or concepts or abstractions, but a texture of metaphors or spirituality. The mortality of art is repudiated. Art is a manifestation of the Spirit and, as such, eternal.

Every aspect of Croce's aesthetics is a debate against tradition. It is true that at times Croce is Scholastic and burdensome. What is surprising is that after all his debates against the naturalistic view of art or against the hedonistic and moralistic aesthetics, so much of the Crocean view of art as spirituality remains fresh. And if we look more deeply into this concept of art as spirituality, we will find a definite corollary: art is intuition-expression. Thus Croce brings to art the deepest conviction that art is the representation of feeling: a feeling that is not superficial but deep, profound, and intense and therefore capable of creating an artistic image. And however his aesthetics may be criticized, it remains the most powerful voice in the world of art criticism, and to this extent the only true explanation of the world of Shakespeare or Dante, Homer or Goethe.

The view of reality as Spirit also permeates Croce's historiography. It is true that in his historical works he speaks of moral afflatus and liberty, but it is also evident that these terms are synonymous with Spirit. As against the Marxists, who explain history in terms of economic forces, materialistic interests, and productive means, Croce sees history as an "ethical-political" discipline. We will clarify this important concept. For Croce, when a people have faith in a certain ideal, there is historical splendor; when a people have no en-

thusiasm in any specific human endeavor, there is dec-
adence. Thus history is not only the history of the
state but also the history of religions, moral institutions, myths, legends, feelings, et cetera. Besides the
tradition of Voltaire and Möser, Croce looks most to
Goethe for inspiration. In Goethe he reads that the
proper, unique, and profound theme of history, the
theme to which all other themes are subordinated,
consists of the conflict between belief and disbelief.
Both Croce and Goethe firmly believe that ethical enthusiasm is the real force of history.

Croce's view of history as moral afflatus or liberty is
the theme of his *History of Europe in the Nineteenth
Century*. Croce abhorred materialists and dictators as
much as he loved freedom, and his analysis of the
whole history of nineteenth century Europe is written
in conformity with this criterion. Here the ideal of
liberty is seen as the concrete cause of history: an ideal
that includes Christian morality, the Stoics' ideas of
love and brotherhood, the concepts of liberty, equality, and fraternity, and an ideal that finds its full expression in the liberal minds of Mazzini and Cavour.
And in this book, he stressed the great virtues of Cavour, the sublime enthusiasm of Mazzini, and pointed
out the abyss between the Italian and the German Risorgimento. Because of these loves and abhorrences,
Croce's *History of Europe* is not only a historical work
but also an artistic achievement. Very notable, also, is
Croce's optimism. In his youth he had been bewil-
dered, sorrowful, desperate; but in this work he embraces the world with love and courage, aware of liberty as the primary source of historical life.

It must be frankly said that among some people this

"liberal view" of history has lost much of its force in the light of many dictatorial forces in the world today. They nowadays reject this claim because they see a reality that does not conform to Croce's historical doctrine. But Croce is not easily vanquished. He will continue to assert that even among those who are slaves, the flame of liberty still smoulders within their hearts, and one day, by destroying or reforming, it will establish the realm of liberty.

Croce's view of reality as Spirit also characterizes his ethics. It must be acknowledged that some Crocean statements are more poetical than ethical: at times he speaks more like Foscolo than like Kant. Yet in holding to the doctrine that morality is not a complex of precepts but spirituality or creativity, Croce is enunciating a vital principle that has many important effects. For if a man is moral not because he obeys exterior precepts but the voice of his conscience or spirituality, the door has been opened to an original ethical doctrine. The recognition that man's personal conscience or individuality is necessary to safeguard the moral world is an important Crocean contribution.

Thus Croce, in the full maturity of his mental powers and firmly upholding his idealistic philosophy, began to re-examine the works of Marx at the end of the Second World War. I say "to re-examine" because Croce was not a stranger to the thought of Karl Marx. Let me elaborate this important point.

Under the influence of his teacher, Antonio Labriola, Croce investigated the thought of Karl Marx in 1895. The result was a definite enthusiasm for the German thinker. He himself states: "This intercourse with the literature of Marxism, and the eagerness with which for some time I followed the socialistic press of Germany and Italy, stirred my own being and, for the first time, awakened in me a feeling of enthusiasm yielding a strange taste of newness to me; I was like a man who, having fallen in love for the first time when no longer young, should observe in himself the mysterious process of the new passion." [1] But he soon went beyond the Marxist ideology. He was more critical than his many contemporaries—men like Sorel, Sombart, Pareto, Pantaleoni, and Bernstein. He was determined not only to apply scientific impartiality but also to evaluate his judgments in the light of concrete particulars. The result was the criticism of Marx's economic theories. The labor theory of value is true, Croce says, for an ideal society but not for a historical one. It is based on the idea that labor is the source of value. In our historical societies, however, labor is not the source of value. Likewise, Croce attempts to show that Marx's theory of the falling of the rate of profit is untrue. Marx, Croce says, evaluates the technical capital of a more advanced society in the light of a less advanced one. Certainly the rate of profit falls in a society that is changing from an agricultural to an industrial one; but in an industrial society that is already established, there is no such decline in the rate of profit. Here it is evident, says Croce, that Marx does not think in concrete terms.

The last three years of the nineteenth century produced a remarkable strengthening of Croce's anti-Marxism. The first manifestations of this were certain

---

[1] R. Piccoli, *Benedetto Croce* (Macmillan: New York, 1922), p. 72.

specific views he expressed concerning Marx's master-piece, *Das Kapital*. In various articles, Croce tried to communicate to Italian intellectuals something of his conviction that the disciples of Marx, and Marx himself, were wrong. A new era of analysis was being born and, with its birth, Croce saw the approaching defeat of Marxist ideology. He called upon the disciples of Marx to consider the following observations: (1) Marx's *Das Kapital* is not a *complete economic work*. Marx's research does not embrace the entire territory of economic facts. It concerns itself only with a particular economic aspect: private property. It does not deal with other historical formations, such as monopolistic or communistic societies. (2) Marx's book is not an *economic monograph of the laws of the capitalistic society*, that is, it is not a theoretical work. Marx, Croce says, was too much of a revolutionary to devote himself to theoretical studies. He was a practical man and, as such, was impatient with any investigation that did not have a strong connection with the interests of actual and historical life. He was neither a philosopher nor an economist but an enthusiastic creator of political ideologies and myths.

Nowadays this treatment of Marx's economic theories and masterpiece, and especially his criticism of the labor theory of value, does not stir us. Yet we must realize how original was Croce's examination of Karl Marx at the time he began his analyses in order to understand the full indignation of the faithful Marxists who assailed him for two generations. To their way of thinking, Croce was not an "economist" but a "philosopher," and that was enough to condemn him. Most of their charges were groundless.

After the First World War, Croce's interest in Marx underwent a definite modification. He now began to see Marxism not as an economic theory but as a materialistic metaphysics. As he says: "The ideal contrast between communism and liberalism, the religious contrast between the two, consists in the opposition between materialism and spiritualism, in the intrinsic materialistic character of communism, in its making God out of the flesh or matter." [2] This materialistic metaphysics or *paneconomismo* has three basic aspects: matter is a metaphysical principle, every spiritual manifestation is the product of the economic factor, and the future belongs to the dictatorship of the proletariat. Of these three aspects, Croce concentrated a bit more on the second because it was the most revolutionary idea in the thinking of Marx. There can be no question of the absolute reduction of history to economics, Croce contended; for history is not the product of economic forces but the effect of freedom. Only when we understand this principle do we understand history and penetrate to its very essence.

As Croce saw it, he had disposed of the economic interpretation of history once and for all. But with the Second World War and with the glorification of Russia's military achievements, Croce was stimulated to enter the arena once more. The result was many essays that he wrote as an integral part of some of his books. This translator has selected the most important ones, and they appear for the first time in English and as a unit with the title, *Essays on Marx and Russia*.

---

[2] B. Croce, *Storia d'Europa nel secolo decimonono* (Laterza: Bari, 1957), p. 38.

These essays reflect Croce's previous positions on Marx and Russia, but there is also something that is definitely new: a novelty that lies in the fact that Croce clearly recognizes the abstract nature of communism: the abolition of the state, the belief in internationalism, economic equality, et cetera. Croce demonstrates that these abstract principles are not and cannot be realized in the only modern state in which communism has had a historical trial, that is, in Russia.

There are some faults in these essays, and no serious student today would adopt his idealistic metaphysics, but Croce's distrust of abstractions is based on a profound ground: the cult of historical reality or concreteness. It is for this intellectual depth and originality, along with his immense culture, that Croce is worth reading after the lapse of two dacades.

                                        Angelo A. De Gennaro

1

OBSERVATIONS
ON ECONOMIC SCIENCE IN RELATION
TO PHILOSOPHY AND HISTORY

Though historical materialism is once again the subject of a great deal of discussion and debate, I still have only one feeling concerning it. It is true that the concept originated a century ago in the extreme deliriums of the extravagancies of the exhausted Hegelian school; nevertheless, I feel nothing but astonishment at the conception of man and his history as the prey of a god or demon (economy) who drags him along, trailing illusions of truth, beauty, moral and religious sublimity, all of which are things of economic substance. I am less astonished that these theories are being repeated today, because I am aware of the great power of parroting, especially if it is practiced by politicians with few theoretical scruples. And Marx, the author of the doctrine himself, was a political agitator very sagacious in this sphere, who, in his whole life, I believe, never posed to himself a problem of truth with a disinterested soul, because he was incapable of the requisite love, enthusiasm, and sacrifice, just as others are incapable of appreciating music or poetry.

But in considering the ideas to be meditated or remeditated upon, I shall note that historical materialism, just as any other similar conception, has been deprived of the condition (or, rather, of the imagination) on which it was based: the idea of the utile-economic, which as a material force places itself against or above the human spirit and even dominates it. My philosophy has redeemed utility from the position of inferiority in which it was usually kept by the diffidence of the old philosophers; it has elevated it as a form of the spirit, equal with other forms, such as knowledge, art, morality, and has related it to those forms.

Hence it is no longer valid to speak of the more or less Manichean dualism of utility, nor of the primacy conferred upon it by historical materialism. By this, philosophy not only integrates itself with a part of itself that had been neglected, mistreated, or badly used; it also re-establishes the harmony between doctrinal systematization and common sense. Is there, truly, someone who, reflecting upon himself at the moment in which he is illuminated by the light of thought, or is enraptured by a poem or a nuance of color, or is excited before the spectacle of the virtues, has not implicitly rejected the materialistic indecency that dares to explain those feelings in the light of economy and, to be sure, of the "class struggle"?

But in my philosophy the elevation of utility to a spiritual form, as autonomous and deserving as the others, and the special philosophy which it creates and in which speculations on prudence, politics, war, and passions are gathered and find their place, has had an ulterior consequence. The result has been the differentiation of this "philosophy of utility or economics" from the "science of economics," and the determination and circumscription of the latter's own character.

Economic science, whether it be pure or political, is not philosophy, though in their discussions many economists are (or were) accustomed to engage in misdirected researches, inappropriate to the subject, on the merits of economic values and their relationship with intellectual, aesthetic, moral, and other similar values. Nor is economic science even a natural science in the same category as zoology or botany or, to be sure, as that science which assumed the name of "sociology" and which the economists justly hold in low regard. The true nature of economic science is applied mathematics, and the former adopts the latter's procedures, quantifying certain kinds of man's actions, converting them into numerable and measurable phenomena and keeping a watchful eye so that the action may take place with numerable and measurable advantage or profit.[1]

Economic science defines the various elements of this economic production, such as capital, work, interest, money, commerce, banks, and so forth; and clarifies the services that each element renders or does not render for the purpose of increasing the production of utilities. Thus economic science brings foresight into the travail of practical life and removes fantasies which are generally baseless; and, at the same time, it eliminates dangerous hopes and fears.

Since simple and handy examples are best, does one not see today how economic science grows weary of explaining that, where there is a scarcity of utilities due to decreased production, the multiplication of paper money increases salaries and wages but diminishes purchasing power because, by means of such multiplication, it is impossible to make available the needed goods? Thus this multiplication, instead of increasing the common welfare, actually increases misery and is, therefore, harmful. Such is economic science, and such is the way it preaches to those who cannot hear or will not listen to it.

Connected as it is with the fortunes of economic production, economic science has initiated its grandiose doctrinal development in the modern age, especially from the sixteenth to the twentieth centuries, which has been avid for discoveries, new markets, technical advances, and industries. Greco-Roman antiquity offers us (as do the Middle Ages) only a few examples of economic activity. In primitive times there was work, and there were technical inventions. But the conditions of economic production were so rudimentary (compared to ours) that economic speculation had less opportunity to develop than philosophical reflection, which took the form of myth and religion; or art, which at times found expression in naive graffiti and bas-reliefs; or morality, which manifested itself in rigid family and tribal customs.

Not that if the course of events continues to develop, as it appears, toward the simplification of regulated economy or, as it is called, planned or state economy, economic science will continue to prosper as it prospered during the last centuries in Europe. Its theorems, like the shining theorem of Ricardo's differential income, will have no more actuality, and will disappear into the realm of erudite researches. A similar fate befell the tribunal casuistry of the feudal law; or, as another example, "the baronial writing of double style" that was still being investigated in seventeenth-century Naples by those preparing to be accountants and administrators for the feudal houses—a tradition that later was disrupted and eventually disappeared. Besides, a foretaste of the destiny awaiting economic science, which has become a science of the state, was given to us a year ago by a German economist, Gott-Ottilienfeld, an apostle of the state economy and a bitter critic of the Western or Ricardian economy (a morbidly refined one, according to him). He saw it as "a circus of goods with acrobatics of values and prices on a mathematical trapeze and with *homo oeconomicus* as clown." [2]

Not only the connection with the various and transient forms of economic production, but also the concentration on certain groups of actions, which lend themselves to quantitative transformation into numerable or measurable things, imposes on economic science severe abstract limitations which prevent it from exercising absolute dominion in its own sphere. Because economic science cannot exercise absolute dominion, it centers its whole attention on the multiplication of certain kinds of goods (called wealth), but it cannot transform its assiduous work of admonition and incitement into an imperative.

Economic science does not have an imperative quality in the eyes of the individual, who at times gives up wealth and material goods and embraces poverty in order to pursue the accumulation of other wealth and goods that have nothing in common with the former ones. And thus the individual belies the cynical saying, "Every man's act has its price," demonstrating by deed that there are things without price. Economic science as an imperative is not even followed by people who, when the occasion presents itself, rather than

keeping the wealth which they have accumulated as
the result of more intensive productive work, throw
everything away in order to actualize their ideals, or
simply their fancies.

The limitation of economic science, and this limitation constitutes its dignity, is felt by its most serious
students. But this does not prevent economic science
from often maintaining theses that are not purely economic—that merely represent the tendencies of one or
another social or political party. Marx fulminated
against the economic literature that in England, after
1830, succeeded the austere science of Ricardo, and
that was defiled by class interests and centered its attention on apologizing for the bourgeoisie and capitalism.[3] But in the meantime Marx himself was writing *Das Kapital*, in which he erred more grievously
than his adversaries because he distorted the very
method of economic science by introducing antieco-
nomic concepts like those of unpaid labor and surplus
labor engendering profit. And all this in order to
create an illusory scientific basis for the political action by the proletariat that he envisioned. The truth
is that, whatever they may be, all the tendencies and
programs of social organization are extraneous to the
essence of economic science; that these programs are
invoked in its name and added to it because of passionate suggestions or political calculation.

The thesis of pure laissez-faire and that of pure stat-
ism and communism are equivalent, as I have already
demonstrated, in the common lack of doctrinal justification; but also in the lack of the infinite intermediate
solutions between these two extremes—solutions that
have been and can be proposed. Why? Because from

time to time in determinate historical conditions the solution uniquely depends on the ethical-political conscience which alone wins over the abstractness of economic science. When recently a capable economist devoted himself to the search for a "third road" between the two and believed he had found it in the economic field itself, in the so-called "market economy," I noted that he was theoretically falling into an error because the "third road" could not be found in a compromise between laissez-faire and communism, but on a higher level to which one must raise oneself.[4]

2

THE DIVERSE BEHAVIOR
OF PHILOSOPHY AND METAPHYSICS
IN REGARD TO PRACTICAL IDEALS

Here is is pertinent to clarify the relationship of philosophy with ideals and political operations.

This relationship is the same as that between thought and action; the first is the necessary precedent of the second. But it is not its cause; for the mind clarifies the situation in which from time to time man finds himself, while only the heart, as they say, suggests the line that a man's action must follow. To espouse practical and political ideals and to act accordingly is the function of the will. The philosopher who is also a historian cannot deduce his own action by means of his philosophy and his historical vision; each action must only emanate from his own soul by the means, and within the limitations, offered him by his practical genius. Thus it happens that men of great philosophical genius become the followers of the man of affairs who possesses to a high degree the genius of action.

Consequently, a philosophy which both embodies an ideal and plans a political action is not a genuine philosophy. Upon closer examination it proves to be nothing but a practical action dressed up in pseudo-philosophical clothes.

How it succeeds in its disguise and in passing itself off as philosophy, as exemplified not only by Marxian disciples but also by its founder, is explained by the confusion between philosophy and metaphysics; between philosophy, which is the critical judgment of reality, and metaphysics, the assertion of the truly real world which transcends reality and governs it from above or from below. The part that feelings, passions, needs, and tendencies play in metaphysics reveals the affinity between metaphysics and religious mythology, the former differing from the latter in so far as it vainly endeavors to be, not a work of revelation, but of thought that defines and formulates concepts. Within every metaphysician there is always the mystic, who is supremely sure of what he asserts but who cannot explain it to profane people who are not touched by grace.

Thus in each of the different varieties of metaphysics is reflected the religious motif of redemption from sorrow and evil, which (as immanent to reality, effort, and achievement in every moment of life) is fancifully projected into a history of the world, of its origins, of its epochs, and of its final form, and which is usually placed in an ultramundane paradise, but also at times in an earthly paradise: variously fancied meditations and combinations that are found again in beliefs and theologies as well as in philosophical systems. It is acutely observed that, differently from the genuine philosophies that distinguish the manifestations of reality, that seek out its relations and unity and have a critical character, the many kinds of metaphy-

sics tend to assume the narrative form and to mold
themselves into a tale of the same character as Genesis.

Hegel envelops his stupendous critical investigation
in a system in which the Idea, or God, creates Himself
through a process of triads that find rest in the final
one; then the Idea resolves to come out of itself, to
place nature outside of itself, and to return from this
alienation to itself by means of Man who, undergoing
a long process of elevation from the purely sensual up
to the Absolute Spirit (that is, philosophy), rests in
God or in the Idea. This Hegelian "metaphysics" pom-
pously obscures the effective contribution that Hegel
makes to "philosophy." The duty of criticism has been
and always ought to be to free this contribution from
the enormous extraneous weight that depresses and
deforms it.

Now it is no wonder that, having kept alive such
metaphysics, such a history of the world from its origins to its predetermined end, Hegel's disciples intended to preserve their master's scheme and method
while interjecting feelings, passions, tendencies, hopes,
certainties, which were very different from those set
forth by him. These were preserved and cultivated by
the so-called Hegelian Right, which was closer to his
teaching, less daring, and less apt to be defeated by
the younger disciples, who belonged to the second gen-
eration, the so-called Left, or the extreme wing of the
school.

Marx and Engels were among these young men;
and they were shocked by conditions among the proletariat who, in the early 1840's, were the object of
protest, threatened revolts, proposed reforms, intensive studies on the part of economists, parliamentary

debates—that whole movement which called itself "communism" and then "socialism." On the other hand, students and ordinary readers of the books of the last great German philosopher, Hegel, participating in the debates which those doctrines occasioned, ended by finding the bond between their political and moral interest and their theoretical and philosophical ones—by pouring into the Hegelian scheme, into its dialectic logic and philosophy of history, their revolutionary ideal, thus acquiring a practical direction to action and giving their revolutionary ideal a form, or pretended form, of philosophical demonstration.

Marx's and Engel's ideology was not mere political shrewdness, a philosophical revolutionary imbroglio, a deceit consciously woven for the purposes of the party, an insidious weapon forged for battle; it was a sincere enthusiasm, a joy in the belief of having discovered a truth of primary importance that would give a new impetus to life and history. And if there was deceit, it was a deceit of which they themselves were the first victims, or, as one usually describes such massive logical errors, a deceit in all good faith. Once that harmony between Hegelianism and communist revolution had flashed into their minds, it was not easy, so great was the fascination of Hegelian thought, for fervent young men to resist the temptation to relive it in themselves and to become its apostles; especially since the time was so far from ripe for a critical revision, of which there was then not even a beginning.

One cannot consider as a truly critical revision the opposition of backward philosophers, an opposition as impotent as that of the initiate who, nevertheless, does not know how to objectify the problems that are being debated. I do not believe that Marx and Engels later became aware of having taken a wrong road, but rather it seems to me that they did not know how to go beyond that on which they had set out in the year 1845; that they did not know how to develop their theory philosophically and not just aphoristically, how to resolve the difficulties that their formulas encountered.

Marx, who, of the two friends, had the stronger and more inventive mind, abandoned philosophy and attempted to elaborate a new economic theory in his *Das Kapital* which, of course, he never finished. And it is very doubtful whether, when much later it was posthumously published by Engels, Marx would have been satisfied with it. Besides, he was always more occupied with the work of the party which had gathered under the banner of his theories. But this work was political work—that is, something different from a banner and requiring a great effort to meet difficulties, to make adjustments, to evolve new formulas, and to do all the other things which are necessary to the life of a party. Philosophically, nothing new was introduced into the live circle of the mental process by the first youthful enunciations. Engels, in his book against Dühring, writes puerile things about logic and dialectic; the other Marxists, mostly simple publicists and political agitators, were arid mouthpieces; and if at the end of the century a philosophical movement was attempted by the German Marxists, it was formulated as an aspiration toward the "return of Kant" (K. Schmidt). Only in Italy did Antonio Labriola [1] try to make historical materialism progress philosophically; but his efforts served rather to point out the shaky foundation of the doctrine.

In our day, in Russia and in the communism one sees as a reality or as an aspiration spread over the modern world, nothing new has stemmed from the primitive nucleus of Marxian thought; it is used today as a formulary, not so much of propaganda, which molds the mind, but as a bludgeon, which stuns the mind and tries to prevent it from thinking. Thus historical materialism, which has lost every trace of mental value, which has decayed into a complex of words without meaning, which has operated to subject the inexpert or the naive and to overpower those who want to see clearly and to reason cleverly, has now become a politician's deceit. This was not so when, in his twenty-seventh year, it was conceived by Karl Marx, and opening to him as it did a source of joy and faith—and by his twenty-five-year-old contemporary and friend, Friedrich Engels. And I can imagine their colloquies about the great secret and the great mental treasure they thought they had discovered; the boldness which affected them; the plans they formed; that fusion of their souls in the great duty to be fulfilled for the palingenesis of human society. And it almost pains me to recall the youthfully bold words that in those times their lips enunciated—words reduced now to a coarse jargon, mechanically and slanderously repeated.

3

THE YOUTHFUL PHILOSOPHY
OF MARX AND THE ARRESTMENT
OF ITS DEVELOPMENT

The translation of Marx's 1844 economic-philosophi-
cal writings, which the Italian scholar Bobbio has
made with admirable care,[1] is timely in the light of
the effort now being made to restore the scientific aspect of Marx; an aspect that has been disfigured ever
since the adoption of his name as a party catchword,
which has deprived it of any other significance. In
these earlier writings of Marx, one finds the sincere
and clear assertion of things that only a sagacious and
expert eye can perceive in the works of his maturity.

What did he want to accomplish, in that philosophical program prepared in the year 1844? Retaining its
framework, he wanted to re-create the Hegelian system by replenishing it with new material and new interests. This was equivalent to accepting the old and
perishable part of Hegel and disregarding that original and extremely fecund, difficult, and still complex
part that is still a part of us. The framework, principle, means, and end were expounded by way of one
of the usual historicoprophecies of the fall and redemption of mankind: an historicoprophecy of the
kind that is found in biblical-evangelical religion.

Therefore Hegel, who shows how the Idea progresses through the logic of all the categories of which it is constituted, how it decides to alienate itself by the creation of nature, and in this alienation ascends to organic life, makes the Idea enter into the life of the spirit through a new negation and return to itself and to its domicile, reinvigorated as it emerges from the two-way trip. Karl Marx wanted us to witness a different journey (but not different in rhythm), beginning with a fall of mankind into the sad adventure of private property: the work of a sort of intangible demon. This adventure consisted of a journey through three stages, of slavery, serfdom, and the proletariat; the last stage being represented, through the negation of the negation, by the advent of the definitive communist era.

These were two different histories of mankind, both methodologically arbitrary, following the same scheme. Of the two, it was the Hegelian that embraced the Oriental, Greek, Roman, and modern or German civilizations, with their religions, their philosophies, and their arts; whereas the Marxian conception renounced all of these, considering them no more than the tools or masks of private property, a conception that deprived of all reality the poetry of Homer and Shakespeare, the philosophical world of Plato and Kant. Even when Marx discussed economic facts, one sensed that they were scarecrows rather than reality, because the private economy and the public one, private property and the common or state property, are two forms which cannot be abolished entirely (nor can the one have priority over the other), but will always persist; and moral values cannot be divided according to the respective conditions of proprietors and proletarians, because each is necessarily born in a certain organized society and within its social structure develops the thoughts and actions that constitute its history. It goes without saying that it was only those who came from what is called the "bourgeois" class who proposed and solicited modifications and reforms in the organization of property, and it was they who conceived communism itself. And the saint who espoused Poverty and provided her with numerous followers was the son of the rich Pietro Bernadone.

To add an example of the inconsistency of this Marxian history, one is invited to observe what is said about the division between the worker and the work that he performs, without enthusiasm, from coercion and, in a word, with sorrow, and whose product is an object that separates itself from its maker and becomes the property of others. Now, even in the most congenial work, like that of the philosopher, who solves the problem of truth, or that of the artist, who creates works of beauty, the moment of sorrow is unavoidable. The philosopher and artist give birth with pain, yet even their product separates itself from them, a deprivation which leaves them inadequate and uncomprehending before it, while others comprehend, appropriate, and develop it, because they themselves are incapable of such accomplishment. For this reason it is well, in history, to look always to the reality of the work, to its life, and not to the reality of its creator, who has identified himself and become one with the work. The worker, like anyone else, cannot create unless he loves his work; and by loving his work he improves and separates it from himself.

All such philosophies—or rather, historicoprophecies—face the impossibility of putting an end to the designated development and of positing an ultimate and determinate reality; and, in effect, it has been endlessly debated whether or not Hegel intended to reduce Christianity, which he had declared "absolute religion," to speculative terms (and Marx, not without foundation, accused him, since he had embarked on a course destined to reach beyond religions, of falling back into them). Marx could never give a precise definition of the communism about which he spoke. However, Marx excluded what he called "crude communism," that is, private property itself which attempts to establish itself as a "political community" and whose characteristic degrading quality is the communization of women: making women the property of the community. He also excluded the political form of communism, which can occur in a despotic society as well as in a democratic one; and, finally, the communism which had "abolished the state" but which had not suppressed private property because it had not "appropriated the essence of man through man and for man." True and proper communism would come about only through a return to the true nature of man, through "man as a social being, that is, human" in an exemplary condition of "materialism" which at the same time would be exemplary "humanism." He defined this as "the true solution of the antagonism between nature and man, between man and man, of the contrast between existence and essence, between objectification and self-assertion, between liberty and necessity, between individual and *genus*" and, in short, the solution—the conscious solution—of the "enigma of history."

I doubt if anyone can make sense of these words;

I also doubt that Marx himself could make sense of
them. The fact that he always avoided elucidating this
point, that he resorted to witticisms and bon mots, is
an indication of his evasion; but, in saying this, I
guard against believing or insinuating that he, a false
prophet, wanted to deceive his followers. Instead, it
seems probable that he must have been thoroughly
convinced of the need to think in terms of a perfect
form of human life and its eventual realization. In
short, he was the prisoner of an illusion.

To the forefront of the political problems confront-
ing the young Marx had come one which, because of
its importance, came to be called the "social question." This "social question" was the real result of
the Industrial Revolution, which, in the marvelous
growth of production and wealth, had brought conditions that were deplorable and in many ways inferior
to those the workers had formerly experienced. Like
so many of his contemporaries, Marx was possessed
with passion and fervor, love and hatred, for the "social question"; but another passion, contemporary and
German, also possessed him: the passion for Hegelian
philosophy. By uniting his philosophical and political
passions, he transformed the one into the other.

But Hegel had really fallen into a great error. He
had given stimulus to a dynamic and historical philosophy through the concepts of dialectic and becoming, but at the same time had suffocated it with a static
construction, a closed and definitive system. And Marx,
though he had departed (or believed he had departed)
from Hegel in other ways, remained strictly bound to
Hegel in this; and he was not troubled by doubt. Here
one sees Marx looking for the perfect social form to

solve the social question. This form was his mate-realistic and humanistic communism in which the Idea conciliated itself with reality, and nature with humanity.

Was this perfect social form admissible? Would this historical form, which theoretically society had created, have been perfect? Was not this concept a contradiction in terms? Can history stop itself and continue to exist as reality? Is not history, perhaps, perpetually reaching beyond itself? If Hegel were mistaken in attempting to create a definitive system, by reasserting its sovereignty, would not the dialectical principle, or dynamic, if you will, which constitutes his glory, throw him to the winds? It did do so; and the history of philosophy itself has refuted the Hegelian concept, that connected the traditional systems by a chain which, going from strength to strength, ended in the perfect system that, by the merest chance, was his own. Now, on the contrary, the history of philosophy is considered as a series of monographs, each of which centers on a new problem occupying the mind of the thinker and investigates the proper precedents and the proper relations; and this form must prevail because it is the only one corresponding to fact.

Thus in every aspect of history the definitive does not exist; nor is the "social question" itself—which still continues to occupy the minds of publicists and the work of parliaments—definitive. This is the historical reality, always "imperfect," as opposed to the perfect form with which Marx thought to solve the "enigma of history" and which is recalled in his youthful pages.

Those early writings also suggest another observa-

tion concerning the doctrines of the then famous economists. Marx's criticisms have a philosophical and
moral characteristic; and economics, even though its
students incidentally show their philosophical and
moral tendencies, is neither philosophy nor morality,
but a method for calculating and understanding the
conditions of economic production. Therefore, though
he fought so hard against them economists generally
let it be known that they were simply misunderstood.
And reasonably so, since his concepts, beginning with
those of "surplus value," did not belong to economic
science but were artificial constructions designed to
support the idea of the Utopia that was fundamental
to his thought.

4

THE HEGELIAN ORTHODOXY
OF MARX

In a noted passage in the preface to the second edition (1873) of *Das Kapital* [1] Marx defines his relationship with Hegelian philosophy by asserting that his dialectic method "is not only different but directly opposite to that of Hegel because in Hegel the process of thought, which under the name of the Idea he transforms into an independent subject, is the creator of reality which is only the external appearance of the Idea." Instead, for Marx "the ideal is nothing more than matter transposed and that has become man's mind." Marx also concedes that "this mysticism which suffers at the hands of Hegel does not minimize the fact that he was the first to expound, in a comprehensive and conscious way, the general forms within which the dialectic moves itself." Hegel, Marx adds, grounded the dialectic in the "world of the mind" and one must "reverse it in order to uncover the rational kernel in the mystic envelope."

But though the Hegelian dialectic truly had need—and this was sensed more or less sharply in many quarters—of an internal reform, Marx never attempted it. This is evidenced by the summing up of his thought which fails to speak of rectifying this or that point of the logical doctrine of Hegel but only

of having substituted the principle of the Hegelian
system, which would be the mental process of Idea,
with the opposite principle of Matter, boasting of the
operation performed by calling it "overturning."
Nevertheless, whatever the metaphysical principle,
whether of Idea or Matter, the logical method adopted
by Marx is intrinsically and organically the Hegelian
one itself; he accepted and applied the Hegelian dialectic, together with the vitiation intrinsic to it, and
thus compromized the firmness and efficacy of his
system.

Perhaps this vitiation had its psychological origin in
the theological and transcendent element which per-
sisted in Hegel's immanentism and which perturbed
his thought. And in Marx this vitiation might have
been the result of an analogous contradictory union
of the realistic element with the one of *natural law*.[2]
Perhaps, more simply, it was the effect of the authority
that Hegel exercised over Marx, and whose scheme of
high logic he adopted. But we are interested in considering and defining this vitiation in its logical form,
whatever may have been the psychological disposition
that caused the error common to both thinkers. In this
logical form the life of the spirit—that it, of reality—
was conceived as a chain process of oppositions transcended by virtue of the conversion of the negative
term into the positive, the latter denying and simultaneously preserving the former: a process that was a
progression from an inferior to a superior degree, up
to a final degree in which the process achieves the fullness of perfection and is there arrested. But though
that process was conceived as progressive, it was always
a sorrowful passage from imperfection to imperfection

and it never achieved in any of its stages, except the last one, the full positiveness of truth, goodness, beauty; and when, in the last stage, the process did achieve the full positivifrom, it denied the life of the spirit, even reality itself, by extinguishing the continuous rebirth of the opposition in which the process itself has its own being, namely, its life. In dialectic logic one witnesses the repetition of the adventure in which the principle of cause finds itself. And those who espouse this principle, and who judge in terms of cause and effect, end with a final cause that is not the effect of any other and they behave (as Schopenhauer acutely pointed out) like one who, after having ridden in a hired carriage all day, arrives home at night and dismisses it at the door.

Probably, as we have already said, because of his theological and transcendent inclination, culminating in the rupture of the process of becoming, his drowning in the contemplation of the Idea and divinization, Hegel was impeded from thinking of the series of the triads as a whole that progresses toward the infinite; from thinking of each triad as finite and perfect in itself, as far as it encloses the infinite in its actuality; from thinking of new oppositions, not as rising from unconquered abstraction and imperfection, still alive in their predecessors, but rather from the wealth of the new life produced by the solution which engenders new oppositions, that is, new problems.

Thus Hegel was unable to penetrate to the depth of the process of opposition and into its resolution, in which he would have found the living and dynamic distinction of the forms or categories that resolution alone engenders. In every stage of development, man possesses and enjoys truth, goodness, beauty, every form of value; and at the same time he starts the process of conquering other values which, though more complex than their predecessors, are homogeneous to them and which, therefore, include them. Thus life develops its true sufficiency and escapes being desperately insufficient, or merely adequate like the death of the spirit which purifies itself and becomes worthy of ascending to heaven by submerging itself in the eternal fountain, into the peace of the Idea, or God.[3]

Marx, who remained essentially an orthodox Hegelian, accepted Hegel's vitiated logic and departed from it only in diverse affection and interest toward certain parts and aspects of history; in purpose and political program, and in the expectation of the future as befitted his revolutionary and neo-communist soul. In Hegel the history of philosophy was essentially progress from the abstract to the concrete: a progress that makes possible an ever-widening approach toward the concrete, but that always remains entangled in the abstract (however gradually decreasing this abstract may be) until it realizes a definitive philosophy that can liberate thought from imprisonment. This state of imprisonment, though it gradually becomes less restricting is, nonetheless, always imprisonment, in which thought remains confined, but at the very moment of its creation it is annulled by a beatitude of which it has no need and which is sublimely obtuse.

In the same way Marx dealt with the economic history of humanity. He saw history in terms of galley slaves whom the hand of the executioner keeps in slavery for several centuries, in serfdom for several more, and in modern times in salaried service. During this succession of ages the serf enjoys less abject conditions than those of the slave, and the salaried proletarian is freer than the serf. But none of them has realized the freedom and dignity that belong to man; all are pressed by necessity, and truly their executioners are tyrants and exploiters and therefore also not free. In the end, by the rebellion of the workers or proletarians against the owners of capital, both classes will disappear (one in the act itself and the other a bit later), because of the resolve of the workers to break the millennial spell. Both workers and capitalists, enfranchised and made equal, without further struggle, without further conflicts, without the structure of the state, and also without the necessity of moral restrictions, will breathe the hitherto forbidden atmosphere of freedom. Morality, like the state, will become superfluous in a society in which the free development of each individual will be the condition for the free development of all.[4]

This is the perfect confirmation of Hegel's history of thought and view of the whole of history, the result of his powerful but vitiated dialectic. It is the denial of the earth for heaven, of the mundane life for paradise and for the inertia of the elect in paradise. Not an inertia for inertia's sake, rather, the elect, as in the story of the tiny angels who have only head and wings and when invited to sit down, *ils n'ont pas de quoi* (they do not have what it takes), have no mental difficulties to resolve, nor sorrows and misfortunes demanding of action.

But there is a difference that should be noted in the catastrophically definitive and paradoxical repose which is the effect of the dialectic of the unilateral opposition, be it in the Hegelian conception or in the Marxian: a difference in the seriousness of the consequences, or, rather, of the practical effects. One may well assert a philosophy that is definitive, but this philosophy takes care to belie itself, as actually happened in Hegel's case. Indefatigable in doubt, thought, and investigation, Hegel, shortly before he died, turned to his wife and sighed: "I cannot make head nor tail of this." And it may be said that art is dead or must die in philosophy; but every poet, every artist born into this world continues to create it with the irresistible force of his genius. The definitive Prussian state of the Restoration may be admired as the ultimate in political life; but dissenters will soon break down that enclosure. The paradoxical conception that crowns Marx's historical vision diverts men from the consciousness of an essential truth and the foundation of the virtuous dyad that is indispensable to life: resignation and courage.

Sorrow and evil are not contingent facts which tormented human society of the past and which the future can erase completely; the joy, the goodness, and the enjoyment of truth and beauty were never denied to the past; but they would truly be denied to the future if life could, according to this absurd concept, realize itself without the torment by means of which from time to time the positive rises from the negative. One need not be discouraged before the Hegelian vision of an historical sequence of philosophers: not all of them enjoyed or possessed the full truth, simply because all of them effectively possessed and enjoyed it fully in the form of a particular truth. As Hegel himself once wittily observed, it is not possible to eat "fruit," but always only an apple, a peach, a plum. Moreover, one must also be careful not to believe in the desolate Marxian vision of history, in which there is nothing but tyranny and exploitation on the part of the few, and abasement or angry impotence on the part of the oppressed and exploited; in which not only the joy of life and the comfort of generosity and virtue are lacking in the world, but also science and poetry, truth and beauty, which, having no function other than that of serving and adorning the interests of the rulers, rarely reflect in their works the voice or a whimper of the oppressed. This vision feeds men with false promises, promises of a state that is unattainable because it is contradictory and takes away from them the clear consciousness that the categories and the dialectic of reality are immortal; that substantially nothing more should be expected from the future than what has occurred in the past. It is not possible to cure the evils of the world with a radical remedy, but only with remedies that have been used and are still in use— among them revolutions which, though they are drastic, are not and cannot ever be a radical remedy.

The real and moral duty of man is another thing. It is to accept, to improve, and to increase, according to conditions that always change, the heritage of our fathers, the heritage of sorrows and joys, of the struggle of good against evil, of the affirmation of truth against falsehood, of sufferings resulting from historical movement. This historical movement, like nature, which is also a historical process, has its adjustments, earthquakes, eruptions, destructions, and periods of calm and relative happiness during which humanity has confidence, though it is not always willing to re-

member it, that that happiness, enjoyed at other times
or by other generations of men, is a haven where it
can save its breath for new sufferings, new labors, and
new misfortunes. People protest strongly against religions which, with the promises of the above, lull man
with vain hopes. Is it then legitimate to cheat him by
rationalistic deception, with promises of the here and
now which are not possible to attain? A virile attitude
toward life is highly esteemed; but is not perhaps the
first gesture of such an attitude to face up to the reality of life as it is, without altering or concealing it,
a reality that truly touches the sublime because it is
always, at its innermost, tragic?

This discussion, which has been occasioned by the
vitiation of the Hegelian dialectic and the servile
Marxian orthodoxy, keeps itself within the logical circle of principles and inferences and does not lean toward either party, firmly maintaining that man, each
man, must operate morally according to his Socratic
demon, his interior voice; that the most various and
contradictory actions, which are the product of the
interior voice, are necessary to the historical course;
that everyone has the duty to understand and to know
the relationship which from time to time conditions
his free operation; but that no one can judge from
above, and, by placing himself outside the operation,
blame and condemn it. Thus one can neither approve
nor absolve it.

But the orthodoxy, the servility of Marx to the Hegelian logic, also manifests itself in another way that
gives greater offense and arouses rebellion in our soul.
This is the destruction of all human values outside the
economic one, because it is destructive, mocking, and

insulting, as we have said, to make truth, poetry, and moral ideality tools of the economic factor. This is also strengthened by the other Marxian statement that being does not depend on ideas but ideas depend on being or "external conditions," as in the writings of the Marxian school where external conditions are understood to be economic facts and class interests. I refrain from relating this blindness to ideal values to the personal and private character of Marx, whom Mazzini saw as a man more full of hatred than of love, nor to his hardness and his sarcasm which strongly evoke his Prussian or Bismarckian qualities. I do not trust such psychological deductions, in which one is deceived or does not know what to think—so much so that men often deceive themselves. I prefer, as I have already said, to understand the error in a logical perspective, leaving aside the psychological approach, more useful to poetry and novels than to history.

Now a similar tendency, if not toward the destruction, at least toward the devaluation or inadequate understanding of all other values except one, also reveals itself in Hegelian and other similar systems: systems that maintain a unique form of value as an explanatory principle. In Hegel this principle was the Idea or Logos, as in other systems it was God; though at times the Idea did not seem to replace God but only seemed an attempt to understand or to define him more sharply; and the tendency of Hegel's system was panlogistic in esthetics, morality, politics, and history, with realistic contrasts or contradictions resulting from his vigorous sense of reality unsubdued by the spirit of static systematism. The fact is that in the supreme sphere, that of the Absolute Spirit, action and morality were transcended, and art, equated with religion, disappeared, perfecting itself in philosophy.

By substituting Matter for the Idea Marx did not, as he boasted, restore the object that had been overturned, but simply replaced one metaphysical entity with another (comparable to the other, if not as well reasoned or deduced). Matter as well as Idea had a hostile attitude toward philosophy: that is, criticism and antimetaphysics. His new entity was Matter; not exactly that of the materialists, but a spiritual category, the vital form, the form of the utile-economic which had no right to call itself Matter. Nor should it have undergone this abasement and mortification.

However that may be, not Marx alone, but other philosophers as well, attempted to replace the Hegelian metaphysical entity with another. Among those who played this game were Hartmann, with the unconscious, and Frohschammer with fancy. But once one admits that Matter, which bore the heritage of the Hegelian Idea and through it of the old God, no other value could confront it and maintain its autonomy. All values had to become, as they did with Marx, ministers, agents, or masks of the economy and of Matter. Hegelian panlogism was succeeded by Marxian paneconomism. To impede the progress of this evil and usurping Marxism in the world of the spirit and history, it is necessary not to metaphysicize the spirit by attributing to it a being different from the one that is its unique and genuine being—that is, the relationship of the particular forms, the unity that does not transcend these forms and consists in their relationship.

But Hegel, who in some ways had left his dialectic headless, initiating it from the opposition that is a necessary moment but is connected with that of the distinction, could not preserve the original and philosophical character, that is to say, the dependent independence (liberty in unity and unity in liberty) of the single forms. Nor could Marx, who had followed and accepted the logic of that dialectic, recognize this character, restricting himself as he did to metaphysicizing differently.

As I have investigated only the metaphysical and "totalitarian" error of the Marxian system in the light of the Hegelian logic, I will not identify Marx's abasement and substantial negation of all intellectual, moral, and esthetic values, along with decadentism, sensualism, and sadism, which ignores and reduces them all to lust and bestiality. Hegel's negation had a religious origin, and the religious trait is also evident in Marx's negation—a fanatic religion which suspects enemies everywhere and against whom it arms itself with distrust and accusations of falsehood and disloyalty. But from a practical point of view the two negations, the decadentistic and the Marxian or historical-materialistic, blend into each other and, if they do not become one, add each to each, both competing to desecrate and destroy whatever is or must be sacred for man.

Above all, the turbid collaboration takes place through the murky concept of the will, or inclination, for power. At this point there is no other remedy than to return to the mental clarity, which is both mental clarity and moral force, to the idea of distinction versus totalitarian confusions which, whatever their origins or manifestations, are despicable because they are stupid, and horrible because they are atrocious.[5]

5

THE IMAGINARY PASSAGE
OF MARXIAN COMMUNISM
FROM UTOPIA TO SCIENCE

I believe I have adequately demonstrated [1] that Marx, who interpreted the Hegelian Idea in a materialistic way, or, rather, an economic way, did not revise that system from a speculative and logical point of view. Marx accepted almost completely and exclusively the antiquated and deteriorating part of Hegel, which, in the final analysis, had a theological origin. In short, Marx accepted that part which modern philosophical criticism has rejected. This criticism, the fruitful product of over a century of controversies and intellectual reactions to Hegel, has clarified the initial error which that powerful Hegelian system had not been able to expunge and which it had espoused and allowed to operate pathologically in its breast.

Now, almost as a corollary to the foregoing, I undertake to demonstrate that still another Marxian boast—that he made the passage from "Utopia to science"—was an illusion. The reason for this boast, which his innumerable disciples repeat, is found in the above-mentioned uncritical acceptance of the Hegelian logical and historical scheme. But, in any case, this assertion is entirely unfounded, because in the depth of his thought, he was and remained a Utopian.

Strictly speaking, of what does Utopia consist? It is commonly said that the Utopia of today will be the history of tomorrow; and in this sense Utopia is nothing but the plan of a possibility that today does not find the necessary means to realize itself that it will find later on. But this is not the true and proper Utopia—whose real meaning is "no place," or (as it is also clear) "outside history," outside every history, outside the conditions of every history. This Utopia denies history insofar as it tends toward cessation, whereas history is movement; and movement is the dialectic of opposites. Every attempt to expel opposites from history is vain. Every conception in which opposites are oppressed is contradictory and empty: Utopian.

And communism, which attempts to rise above all forms of social inequality is itself similar to Hegel's Absolute Spirit, which wants to rise above all forms of intellectual suffering and to abolish, in its achieved purity, that same suffering. Communism is a Utopian conception because its inward reality would no longer be "living," as in Hegel the spirit would no longer be "thinking."

And Marx, especially, remained loyal to the recent and popular Utopia of his time, the Utopia of the Owens, Saint- Simons, Fouriers, Cabets, and others, men whom he very much loved, and always defended, and urged his friend Engels [2] to defend, though he excused them for not having yet, because of the immature development of capitalism, realized the passage from the "weapons of criticism" (to use his phrase) to the "criticism of weapons," that is, to criticism converted into a material weapon. Certainly, on this point, he never liked to express himself too clearly, and to the best of his ability avoided all those who were embarrassing him with regard to the character and structure of the future society that would rise after the suicidal victory of the proletariat, a class which, as the result of having annihilated all classes, would die itself.

At times he resorted to witticisms in order to free himself from the embarrassment in which he felt himself caught. He also said, for example, that he was not writing lists for the restaurants of the future. But the characteristic of this postulated society, of this *neue Menscheit* (new humanity) arising from *rücksichtlose Kritik alles Bestehenden* (merciless criticism of whatever exists) (customary words of his by 1843), has no reality. This lack of reality is easily deduced from assertions that in that society the state would be abolished; there would no longer be any civil or penal law, nor any contrast among individuals or groups because the free development of each individual would be the condition for the free development of all. In short, Paradise, in which man would be freed from sweat of the brow and anguish of the heart, would come to earth.

He who meditates on these assertions can find a corollary in the most naive dreams of modern anarchists. But perhaps he will do better if he searches for precedents in the Utopians of the beginning of the nineteenth century, in Saint-Simon with his technical government succeeding the political one, and especially in Fourier, who in the social world had discovered the attraction *qui vient de Dieu* (which comes from God) rather than the restrictive and Kantian duty *qui vient des hommes* (which comes from man). Fourier states that just as Newton had discovered the attraction in the planetary realm, so had he discovered *l'attraction passionée* (the passionate attraction) in the social world; this *attraction passionée* takes various forms, among which the *papillonne passion* (the philandering passion) is not omitted; therefore, in the new society each individual, at his pleasure, may choose whatever occupations he likes, and, twenty if he likes twenty, twenty different ones.

One might amuse oneself by tracing in the writings of Marx, during his formative period, these vestiges of Fourier. In Marx's *Die Deutsche Ideologie,* which belongs to the 1845–1846 period (a work in which he and Engels fixed their philosophical-historical conception), one reads, contrary to the modern necessity for the division of labor, that in a communist society, where general production is regulated, there will be no need for specialists, and the individual will be able to be this or that: in the morning, a hunter, in the afternoon, a fisherman, in the evening a shepherd; and, indeed, Marx adds, a culinary [3] critic when he is not hunter, fisherman, or shepherd, according to his mood. This idea, if I am not mistaken, is exactly what Fourier called the *papillonne passion.*

But if the essence of Marx's thought remained that of the Utopians,[4] in what did he differ from them, such that made him believe that he had passed from Utopia to science? It was not simply that Marx had banished the method of persuasion, propaganda, and example, professed by the communist Utopians; nor because he had adopted the method of violence according to the tradition of Babeuf [5] and to the then practice of Blanqui.[6] It is true that Marx also permitted the momentary use of violence, but only in the manner of the midwife who delivers the fully developed infant; that is, the intervention of violence to execute the death sentence on what has already been condemned by history.

His concept was based on the theory of the philosophy of history borrowed from Hegel. The Marxian theory used the same Hegelian procedure, and if the Hegelian scheme proceeded by epochs logically deduced one from the other, in Marx the historical epochs were not differentiated according to the degrees of liberty, as in Hegel, but according to the degrees of economy. And here the protagonist was not Germanism but the proletariat, which had to bury the bourgeoisie, just as the bourgeoisie had buried feudalism, and as feudalism with its serfdom had, in their time, done away with the old economy of slaves.

This metaphysical construction, as it has been said, of theological origin, these certain a priori previsions (Labriola called them "morphological" previsions), and this deteriorating Hegelianism, of which Marx and his servile imitator Engels proclaimed the German proletariat [7] to be the heir, are what he was calling "science"; and by this non-science—but metaphysics in its purest form—he deluded himself into believing he had placed communism on solid bases, into believing reasonable the opposition of its scientific character to its antecedent, utopianism. Communism was not a social form once possessed and now to be reacquired, nor was it, according to him, an ideal to be realized, but *die wirkliche Bewegung* (the actual movement) which history realizes on its own, by its own intrinsic logic.[8]

Marx was always very rigorous and meticulous in criticizing and opposing every attempt to skip one of the degrees of transition that he had deduced as necessary; and above all he was opposed to the impetuous and anachronistic revolutionism which then refused to ally itself with and give support to bourgeois radicalism and its desire for liberal institutions. The bourgeoisie, according to Marx, had to achieve this improvement in order to make possible its being overthrown by the proletariat. And likewise Marx deplored the impatience of those who did not want to wait for the maturation of the proletariat to such vigor and awareness as would enable it to succeed the bourgeoisie and create the new society.

Thus, Marx took on the semblance of a moderate and a conservative in comparison with the Bakunians, who were always ready to expose themselves to danger. Nevertheless, he was either a conservative nor a moderate, but if anything, a pedantic believer in and an observer of the old Hegelian logic and metaphysics of history. And Mazzini was wrong in his famous judgment on Marx in which he charged him with a lack of "profound philosophical convictions," convictions which, though of the quality already mentioned, were, in their own way, deep and tenacious.

But history is moved by liberty careless of the schemes (which fancy, not thought, constructs) of future manifestations, and of the rhythm and tempo through which it will see them realized; and Marx, in the forty years of his political life, had to pay with many delusions for the notion, expressed in the *Communist Manifesto,* of the imminent catastrophe and end of the bourgeoisie, and of the rapid leap from the

Kingdom of Necessity to the Kingdom of Liberty, to
the Paradise of a more or less Fourierian attraction
and harmony.

I shall not re-create, nor shall I summarize, the history of his political work, starting with his first association with communist groups; his direction of the
review *Neue Rheinische Zeitung;* his participation in
the German revolutions of 1848 and 1849, moving to
the foundation and then dissolution of the International; and to the programs of Gotha and Eisenach.
All of this may readily be found in books.[9] I only want
to note that at no time did Marx pass or fall from the
dialectical method of the old Hegelianism into the
mechanical and deterministic one; as when, for example, he expected a renewal of the general revolutions
of 1848, which he attributed to the great economic
crisis preceding that political crisis, to stem from a
new sequence of world economic (and therefore political and revolutionary) crises—an expectation similar
to that of the legendary crow that returned no more.
It goes without saying that in the years following
Marx, as much as Hegel, took great pains to patch up
the theories of historical materialism and to accom-
modate them to the actual circumstances subsequent
to 1848.

Perhaps it would be worthwhile to reexamine the
oft-debated and variously answered question of his
theory of surplus work and surplus value, and profit
arising from work not paid. This has been disparately
judged—now as independent from morality, now as
of moral origin. The question might be better answered in the light of the manner in which Marx arrived at that doctrine. In contrast to the essence of

economic (and therefore now forgotten) science, he made a mere objective comparison between two different types of the organization of property: the individualistic and the collectivistic. Though this comparison, considered in itself, was formally economic and sociological, the intent for its construction was undoubtedly moralistic; that is, the intent was to formulate and confirm the accusation that capitalism is a structure dishonestly exploiting the workers, morally complementary in character to the doctrine of historical materialism.[10] Besides, *Das Kapital* was conceived and executed when Marx had already elaborated, without reference to that genesis of the origin of profit, the materialistic conception of history.

Such analysis of the origin of profit was wrong, as was also historical materialism as a theory of history. However, both constructions had—and still have—great efficacy as oratorical propaganda. In the world of propaganda, what is said does not necessarily have to be true, but it is necessary that it strike man's imagination and excite his soul. For Marx it was enough for the weapons of criticism "to materialize themselves," that is, to convert themselves in their turn to the "criticism of the weapons." For these reasons, in my earlier book on Marx, more than fifty years ago, I minimized the value of his thought, admired his political genius as a revolutionary, and greeted him as the "Machiavelli of the proletariat," all but a counterpart of that Machiavelli who was an adviser and glorifier of the principality that favored Italian unity and independence.[11]

And now far be it from my intention to deny or to diminish the extent of his influence on the history of

our times; an effect which, if it has not engendered
the new communist society, no man, nor work, having
the strength to change into a fact what is merely a
Utopia, has certainly contributed to generating an
event of as great an importance as the Russian Revolution, an event that creates or has created agitations
and revolutions in other countries. Perhaps Karl Marx
would be amazed if he could see what has developed
in Russia and in other parts of the world under the
aegis of his name and his formulas; perhaps he would
also regret it because he truly lived, at least in his
youth, the dream of a society of such perfection that,
in spite of the ontological argument of Anselm,[12] he
even sacrificed the predicate of existence for it. The
enthusiasm and ardor of the believer, and the unshak-
able persistence of the apostle, that made him devote
his whole difficult life to the effort of translating that
dream into action, cannot go unrecognized, either in
him or in his faithful and worthy friend, Friedrich
Engels.

My indignation glows not against him, though I am
forced to refute his theories in the light of the truth;
nor, as is obvious, against Russia, which, instead of
practicing a humanity-redeeming communism, threatens us (obeying the destiny that orders her) with Pan-
Slavism, the Pan-Slavism once personified by czarism
and which classic Europe abhors, seeing in it its own
death and the death of civilization. Obviously also my
indignation is not directed against the working class,
which, like any part of society, tries to improve itself
even though the communist road it takes has not led
—nor will it lead—either to economic comfort or to
that realistically impossible goal of equality; nor

against that movement which was born simultaneously with liberalism and which, in order to differentiate it from communism, was precisely called "socialism" and which has been operose and beneficial during the course of the nineteenth century.

My indignation turns solely toward these destructive "intellectuals," these Italian or foreign professors who for many years have not been aware of Marxism (which also has had a long history) and have now given themselves to the communist mania and celebrate and inculcate and administer it in their false writings because it seems to them that fortune has crowned and mitered it in Russia.

Among all the European countries, Russia is the country with the sparsest traditions of thought, and of the methodology of thought, and with the poorest record and discipline in this spiritual sphere; and Marx himself never thought that Russia would be the first to create a society like that of which he dreamed. If he had any prevision, it was directed toward England, the leader in industrial development. Nor did Marx think Russia would be able to create an economic science, whose primogeniture he attributed to Germany. In 1829 a Russian, Peter Tschadaïef, noted the profound mental weakness of his people, resulting in the secular estrangement in which they had remained in relation to Greco-Roman culture and the Renaissance, and even to the logical education of medieval scholasticism, so that (Tschadaïf wrote) *"le syllogisme de l'Occident nous est inconnu."* And therefore he cried out: *"Où son nos sages, où son nos penseurs? Qui est-ce qui a jamais pensé pour nous? Solitaire dans le monde, nous n'avons rien donné au monde, nous*

*n'avons rien appris au monde, nous n'avons pas versé
une seule idée dans la masse des idées humaines, nous
n'avons en rien contribué au progrès de l'esprit hu-
main, et tout ce que nous est revenu de ce progrès,
nous l'avons defiguré!"* [12] (Where are our sages? Where
are our thinkers? Who has ever thought for us? Soli-
tary in the world, we have given nothing to the world,
we have taught nothing to the world, we have not
poured one single idea into the mass of human ideas,
we have in no way contributed to the progress of the
human spirit, and whatever we have received from
this progress, we have disfigured!)

Here these professors tire themselves out superim-
posing volumes, pamphlets, and catechisms (I do not
think that they know all these books first-hand and
without bias) onto their texts of Marx and Engels, with
which they are scarcely familiar. But the volumes,
pamphlets, etc., are the product of minds foreign and
rebellious to speculative, historical, and critical research: minds of great capacity and political force like
Lenin and his successor Stalin (the much more cultivated Trotsky is never mentioned); and soon one must
expect, using the same criterion, the addition of those
scientific authorities, Vishinsky, Molotov, and Marshal
Timoshenko. The vanity, the laziness, the fashionable
servility, the *arrivisme,* the obtuseness (with rare ex-
ceptions) of the professors has produced such result:
the professors whom, due to my long experience, I
consider to be incorrigible. It is, however, for this reason that they are to be pointed out: so that they may
be known for what they are, and may not intervene to
waste the time of those who devotedly dedicate themselves to the study of the truth.

6

THE CONCEPT OF CLASSES
AS REAL ENTITIES

For a century, but especially in the last fifty years, the world seems to have been invaded, agitated, obsessed, and frightened by a fury of fantasms, by a sort of medieval band of "hellequins" or "harlequins," by a cavalcade of devils called "social classes." The author or chief begetter was Karl Marx, about whom critical thought must definitely conclude that he was certainly a Semitic prophet of revolutions and a powerful mover of social forces, who, nevertheless, was deprived of vigorous philosophical and scientific genius, which is the genius of truth.

Therefore in the field of philosophy as well as of economics he propagated a series of monstrous concepts, from historical materialism, with the theory of "superstructures," to that of "surplus value" in economic production. Undoubtedly before Marx one spoke of classes in a purely empirical sense; they were the object of exaltations and slanders, delusions and hopes. And if in the Middle Ages the "satire of the villeins" flowered, in modern times that of the aristocracy and then of the bourgeoisie followed. Marx, however, made the social classes rigid and solidified them in dialectical and even metaphysical categories. This was

the distortion he perpetrated and to which he gave a
certain respectability: a distortion which, if it had any
beneficent influence upon the history of thought, it
was that of having, as a reaction, resurrected and re-
juvenated the genuine theory of human history and
pure economic science. Everyone knows what, through
Marx, the important concepts of the feudal aristocracy
became, and how it has been necessary to rectify them
or rather to dissolve them in order to replace his myths
with the realities disfigured by his hateful bitterness
and arrogant definitions.

I offered this revision, resolution, and rectification
in a former essay,[1] examining historically the multiple
meanings of "bourgeois"—which range from the lowly
implication, a mediocrity of the mind and soul, from
the politically and morally serious one, its mediative
function, to that other very lofty conception, a bearer
of culture and civilization. Only as a result of a myth-
ical-metaphysical construction, have people come to
believe that the natural and empirical class designations of the components of society actually exist; that
they are differentiated in good and bad, ungenerous
and generous, sick and healthy classes, transferring to
them the judgments usually given to the social and
moral struggle of individuals and their actions in specific and transient historical situations. I have hinted
at the analysis of the concept of the bourgeois, of
which I have spoken elsewhere, but it is useful to center our attention on those concepts of peasants and
workers, and in general on those of the so-called proletariat, whereby we may observe pessimistic qualities
similar to those of the bourgeoisie.

I will not recall the descriptions and characterizations given to us by the sociologists and realistic or naturalistic novelists like Balzac and, especially, Émile Zola. The latter aroused the indignation and reaction of Marxist writers (among others, those of the *Neue Zeit*) who accused him of being the slanderer of the proletariat in the service of the bourgeoisie: the most unjust accusation ever uttered, considering the undoubted good faith of the writer and his purpose of scientific impartiality. If in the *L'Assommoir* and in *La Terre* he portrayed the vices of the workers and the ferocious greed of the peasants, in *Le Ventre de Paris* he represented the vices of the commercial bourgeoisie, and in *L'Argent,* of the business community. On the other hand, in his *Germinal,* Zola endeavored to portray the ethical motivations of the workers and their struggles, and was a very sincere humanitarian dreamer, as he reveals more and more in his later novels. It is well to remember the judgments of Maxim Gorki, the Bolshevik revolutionary, who in his last years described in darkest tones the class which, in the Russian Revolution, was awarded with triumph over the nobles and landowners. He portrayed the peasants' anarchic, antisocial, anticivic, and antigovernmental character; their immersion, eating the most and working the least, in their own animal egoism; their profound aversion toward the workers, toward the city and culture, of which the workers are the expression; the complete lack of history and tradition of their past; their innumerable superstitions and the absence of ideas; their savage cruelties perpetrated in cold blood during the Revolution (the peasants were not incited by the intellectuals, but acted in spite of the intellectuals and politicians); their religious indifference.

Gorki, therefore, did not foresee any progress on the part of the peasants except as a class of business people whose business would relate exclusively to their own particular interests. For Gorki the figure of the good peasant, who has a spontaneous feeling for truth and justice and human piety, was the literary "invention" of the "friends of the People" against which the Chekhovs and the Bunins protested (see *passim* his book on *Lenin et le paysan russe,* French translation, Paris, 1924). Judgments of this sort are not based on the true nature of human beings but on the concept of "classes," and all judgments on classes tend to become pessimistic because in those schemes human reality is made material and fancifully uniform, entirely subject to the determinism of a cause that cannot be but the stimulus to defend and to promote its own way of life, to realize its own welfare, neglecting every other consideration and every other affection.

As has been said, descriptions of all the other classes of the bourgeoisie, aristocracy, workers, soldiers, priests, etc., lead to the same conclusions. Truth, justice, goodness, generosity, religiosity, beauty, exist in all classes, *nec cubant in ulla* (nor do they reside in any; i.e., in any one alone); they exist in men and not in schemes, and they form the history of humanity, the tradition of mankind, its glory and strength; whereas abstract determinations (classes) end by assigning function and crushing weight (importance) to the passive and negative term (evil) that the human spirit always finds before itself and that it continually reduces to its matter (instrument). Here is the logical error of the class vision of history and human life, by means of which true and full reality is replaced by a monstrously unhistorical history, moved by fanciful entities; and each class is foolishly seen in the light of its own interests or utilitarian acquisitions, closed to all others and inhuman toward common humanity.

But an entirely different spectacle opens itself before the historian who looks with an unbiased eye and sees that humanity affirms itself and develops, grows and restores and tirelessly renews what is called culture, through the concepts of the mind: religious fervor, poetical creation, acts of sacrifice and heroism, useful technical inventions. And the authors and promoters of all these works are not "classes" but individuals, who, it may be said, originate in all the classes, not less from those which are reputed to be the most humble and oppressed, than from others. The glories of the sons of peasants—philosophers, poets, painters, musicians, inventors, statesmen, and leaders of armies—who occupy the first rank in every aspect of social life, need not be recalled to memory.

Modern historiography, after an interval of arid, monotonous, foolishly materialistic, and class-conscious historiography, has again spontaneously taken the natural and traditional road; and in this it gradually and greatly enriches itself through its consciousness and self-assurance. Its future is well assured because it is entrusted to the critical spirit, to the intelligence and feeling of humanity, and is reverent toward its laborious and noble past. Once in our Socratic conversations, and at the time of the delirium over historical materialism, Antonio Labriola, opening to me the very heart of his thought, said: "Essentially, Marx has demonstrated that the history of humanity has for millenniums been that of the wretches —worthy also of compassion—whom hunger and greed have tyrannized in all their acts and in all their struggles and whom hunger and greed continue to tyrannize in their beliefs, thoughts, and virtues, which are nothing but illusions. Its true history, which will be history without distinctions and antitheses of classes, must yet begin!" Into such blindness and confusion had classism and historical materialism thrown even the intelligentsia.

Much more serious, because more directly harmful in the theoretical and historical field, is the peristent conception and posing of political and moral problems, not in the light of creative men and their works, not in the light of humanity's eternal progress, but from the theoretical standpoint of classes (or "masses" as they are also called), resulting in a mechanical vision of life. Hence, instead of directing all the forces of the mind and heart toward searching for and procuring those things which from time to time concur to uplift men to a higher level of humanity, one asks oneself what the masses demand and what the masses want and searches for the mechanical device that will produce this or that effect.

That the masses and classes are abstractions, and therefore incapable of thought and accomplishment, much less of worthy thought and deed (which are only achieved by he who gathers to himself the concreteness of humanity: by the individual) is beyond all doubt; and by a curious manipulation, the thought and will of the demagogues (who claim to speak and desire in their name) are lent to the classes and masses. These demagogues, moreover, have an undoubted advantage over classes and the masses because they themselves are men of flesh and bones, and, therefore, they too are actors, be they great or small, of high status or low, in the passage of history.

The intention here is not to minimize whatever role the demagogues play in history: even they are necessary for certain purposes and perform certain services. Rather, the sole intention is to recommend to those who are not demagogues, who think and desire with a deeper preparedness and greater purity of intention, always to speak and to act not in the name of classes and the masses but as individuals, dictated by what their minds and their hearts discover, propose, and promote for the common good of man, ever anxious for the welfare of all, in their living and individual reality, which is not the fictional reality of classes.

7

OF AN EQUIVOCAL HISTORICAL CONCEPT: "THE BOURGEOISIE"

In reading the works of modern historiography and in noting the use and the abuse that is made of the concept of the "bourgeoisie," and feeling a sense of dissatisfaction and contrariety, many times a thought has occurred to me, to which I have finally decided to give a determinate form: it is necessary to get rid of that concept.

I intend to say that we should get rid of that concept in that sense and not in others. Other legitimate concepts expressed by the same word should be retained.

Thus the *juridical* concept of the "bourgeois" in medieval history, and also in some centuries and some countries of modern history, where it designates the citizen of the *bourg* and of the non-feudal city or the component of one of the "states" of ancient political organization, is perfectly legitimate. And similarly the *economic* concept of the "bourgeois" can be legitimate when it indicates the owner of the means of production, that is, of capital in opposition to the proletariat or salaried persons. It is true that in this second case it would be useful to replace it with the more correct term "capitalist" and not let it fluctuate in representations formed with other and different characteristics. The result is that one often ends by including with the bourgeoisie—and excluding from the proletariat or class of salaried persons—professional men, scientists, literary men, because of their way of life and the quality of their work, while, economically, the difference between them and the so-called factory workers is very slight or even nonexistent. Finally, it would be well to concede that in a *social* sense the term "bourgeois" is used for what is neither too high, nor too low, the "mediocre" in feeling, customs, thought.

The historical concept of the "bourgeois" and "bourgeoisie," which is the object of my negative criticism, is, instead, what one usually means by an entire spiritual personality and, correlatively, an historical epoch in which such a spiritual formation dominates or prevails. Here one deals neither with the juridical subject, nor with the economic subject, nor with an empirical social distinction, but with the moral subject. And, because every morality has as its foundation a conception of life, one comes into contact with a certain religion or philosophy, a complex of convictions and ideas which, even though it is not static, but is in motion and therefore subject to change and development, follows a general direction and obeys a principle or its own principles. In this sense the concept of the "bourgeois" is widely used in modern historiography and becomes the subject of investigation in special monographs of which, in order to concentrate our attention on some examples, I shall mention one written by Sombart [1] some fifteen years ago, and one by Groethuisen [2] more recently.

Now, in the sense outlined above, one may say that

concept is born deformed; that is, it is not the result
of a purely historical consideration but of a practical
polemic: an economic, political, moral polemic carried on by two opposite factions against the society
and the new ruling class that emerged from the French
Revolution. On the one hand, the new social structure
was regarded contemptuously by the aristocrats and
the supporters of the old regimes, who hated it from
the bottom of their offended interests and their whole
beings. On the other, it was looked at askance and
with envy by the proletarians and workers. Their
spokesmen, or rather those who wanted to make themselves interpreters and representatives of the workers
—the socialists—measured the new social structure in
the light of their ideal of a communist society, and
condemned it in the name of the more or less near
future, as the aristocrats did in the name of a more or
less remote past. Both of these groups created the concept of the "bourgeois," of the "bourgeois era" or
"bourgeois civilization," portraying it in colors that
conformed with their feelings of aversion and with
the purpose of their polemics.

This concept, pseudohistorical and intrinsically polemical, was formed in France in the first half of the
nineteenth century and preserves its French imprint in
the word itself, the corresponding words of other languages, in addition to the old meaning, taking on the
French one. Moreover, among the Germans, since the
linguistically corresponding word "bürger" does not
lend itself to the new meaning, and therefore is felt
to be somewhat inadequate, it is at times directly replaced by the French form "der bourgeois," which
appears in the title of Sombart's book. Perhaps the

man who most contributed to the pseudohistorical concept and to the use of the word was Saint-Simon, in whom, it seems, the two contrary aversions of the old aristocrat and of the new apostle of socialism united.

Thus the concept of "bourgeois" and "bourgeois epoch" insinuated itself into modern historiography, and was elevated to the position occupied by "Romanism," "Classicism," "Christianity," "Catholicism," "Protestantism," and other similar terms; then, as the hidden motivation of the spiritual manifestations of the modern age, it slowly began to prevail over all the others. To this modern age were then added the analogous divisions of the ancient economy and civilization of slavery, and of the medieval and feudal era with its serfdom and closed corporations: an ulterior elaboration that was the product of the growing socialistic polemic, and in a more energetic way, of its pseudoscientific and pseudo historical manifestation, that is, Marxism or historical materialism. Furthermore, even today throughout Europe, may be observed, in the use of that concept, the double current that generated it; that is, beside the socialistic, communistic, and even anarchic current, there is the aristocratic and reactionary one that expresses itself in the various nationalisms, with their companions: longed-for absolutism, reestablished nobility, reestablished Catholic discipline.

It should be noted that, while the conception of the bourgeoisie as a spiritual figure and historical epoch was emerging, in the world of social and political polemics and in the country where these polemics were more vivacious and open, the best modern historiog-

raphy, created by idealistic philosophy, especially in
Germany, felt no need for and completely ignored
that concept. Instead, it conceived history as the history of thought or religion, or the progressive consciousness and actualization of liberty, etc., and divided it into epochs indicating the various stages of
this development, such as Theocracy, Classicism, Christianity, Humanism, Reformation, Rationalism, Enlightenment, Romanticism, etc. And, certainly, when
historiography was infused with the arrogance of various peoples such as the Greek World, the Roman
World, the Latin World, Celticism, Germanism, etc.,
each of these "spirits of the peoples" *(Geist der Völ-
ker)* was viewed as the carrier of spiritual values or
systems of those values that were more or less complete
or were moving toward completeness.

Because of the polemical and biased origin of the
concept of which we are speaking, one must consider
as ill-founded and scarcely cautious the method of
modern historiography, which consists of seeking out
the characteristics of the bourgeois and of the age during which it is predominant, how this age began, and
its course, thus peacefully admitting the reality of that
bourgeois form and that age; while, in every case, it
would be pertinent to reexamine the presupposition itself and, at least, to purge it of its polemic scoriae and
to correct it in a critical way, not even excluding the
hypothesis that criticism may lead directly to its dissolution. This is my thesis.

In effect, the aristocratic and reactionary polemic
gave the impression of identifying the bourgeois with
the capitalist, with the speculator, with the rich shop-
keeper, and then also with the politician and the dem-

agogue and other types that became well-known characters in novels and comedies. But if the intrinsic thought of the polemic is examined, and all its offshoots, from end to end, are encompassed, it reveals itself as the negation of the entire civilization that has developed in the modern age.

The polemic was indeed hostile toward the exaggerations, the deficiencies, and the rudenesses that are in every man and every human society, that qualitatively vary with the variation of these and that must necessarily be opposed and repressed as much as possible. The polemic was also hostile toward modern philosophy, which had destroyed and replaced theology; toward the criticism which had dissolved and was continuing to dissolve the dogmas; toward the liberal organization of the state, which set itself against the authoritarian one; toward the liberal competition which had begun its opposition to the mercantile and protective systems; toward the mobility of wealth versus the immobility of the primogenitures and of the fideicommisa and other bonds; toward the techniques which were upsetting the old habits; toward the demand for the new comforts, which necessitated the pulling down of old castles and other buildings, and the rebuilding and enlarging of old cities; toward the democratic feeling which was measuring man with the only measure of pure humanity, that of intellectual and volitive energy. And very often the aristocratic and reactionary polemic spoke clearly and, beyond the bourgeois or in the bourgeois, taken as a symbol, saw as its main enemy modern rationalism, incredulity or disbelief, and individualism; and placed the responsibility for this on the great men, Luther and Descartes,

Calvin and Bacon, Voltaire and Rousseau, and then also on Kant and Hegel and all the others.

Thus, to accept the concept of the bourgeois age is to be trapped by this pseudohistory, a trap one could avoid if, putting one's cards on the table, one revealed the serious image of the entire modern age hidden under the more or less satirical, unattractive, and comical portrayal of the bourgeois.

The fact that the reactionary polemic and its historiography hated, ridiculed, and denied the bourgeoisie, testified to the impotence of this historiography, to its pseudohistoricism; because true history does not deny but rather justifies, does not reject but explains, does not recognize legitimate sons alone, but also bastard and degenerate sons who, whether they are liked or not, will in their turn have progeny, progeny, too, who may be admired by those who, having censured their parents, in this way contributed to the character of that progeny, making themselves spiritual coparents.

This mistake of rejecting and denying the so-called bourgeois age and culture as the worst human manifestation was not shared by socialistic criticism and historiography because of the fear of being thought reactionary. They aspired to go not toward the past but beyond the present and the past. Hence socialism finally assumed an anti-Utopian, critical, or scientific form, or whatever it came to be called, and certainly an economic or materialistic-historical form, as opposed to the fantasies of the Golden Ages and related Utopias. This divergent attitude is sufficiently revealed by the portrayal of the bourgeois age in the *Commu-*

nist Manifesto, by the concluding eulogy and necrology of that age, which are like its lyric or epic.

But if in this way socialism avoided the antihistoricism of the reactionaries, it fell into a different error of historical judgment. In socialism the bourgeois was portrayed as an essentially economic reality; and however much the bourgeois was satirized, his exaggerations and deficiencies, his vulgar and rougher aspects, his hardness and hypocrisy as exploiter, like the bourgeois described by Fourier and whom Marx depicted as "the Knight of the Sad Countenance," he was not confined entirely to that limited role. In socialism the idea of the bourgeois age was widening and evolving into that of the whole modern age, of geographical discoveries, industry, machines, Protestantism, Rationalism, Encyclopedism, and the Kantian philosophy. Therefore socialism intended to transcend the bourgeois age, not only by means of a different organization of economic production, by the abolition of private capitalism, but also by a total transformation of thought and custom, by a new philosophy, a new moral feeling, a new art.

It does not matter that all these things, with an arbitrary and imaginary assertion, were made to depend on and alter with the changing economic structure; what matters is that these things were also included in the socialistic vision and in its predicted and desired revolution. Historical materialism wanted to be precisely a new philosophy and not mere economics (*Das Kapital* is only a fragment of the vast work planned by Marx), a doctrinal motif taking form from a new conception of reality and life. In this sense En-

gels attempted to develop this motif, especially in the
Antidühring: the Engels who proclaimed the proletariat to be the direct "heir" (and therefore conservative and negative and transcending agent) of the "German classic philosophy" and who was not far from the
thought of proletarian ethics, logic, dialectic, phenom-
enology, and, I was going to say, mathematics!

Toward this end Antonio Labriola worked in Italy
for many years; in this sense Sorel dreamed of the new
morality and a new custom for which the workers'
syndicates would plant and cultivate the seeds, somewhat in the manner of the primitive Christian eccle-
sia. Not everyone has forgotten the illusions, which,
thirty years or more ago, were ignited everywhere
(even in Italy), of a socialistic science and art in opposition to the bourgeois science and art, already de-
spised in the name of the imminent future. And should
one forget them; what the Bolsheviks naively attempt
in Russia with their educational institutions and their
"schools of poetry" should help to revive one's memory.

But the fact is that such a new philosophy, new religion, new morality, new custom, new science, new
proletarian art, were empty desires and not reality,
words and not concepts; and they could not humble
the corresponding bourgeois manifestations, with the
exception, perhaps, in theory, of the economic organization of production, because those other manifestations are not only bourgeois or economic but variously
human and therefore speculative, aesthetic, moral.

Art, science, etc., do not tolerate being surpassed except in their own world and for intrinsic reasons, and
in that world they continually surpass, enrich, individ-

ualize, transform themselves, but do give no indication of ever abandoning their leading principle, that which has been taking form and has been purified throughout all history, and which, during the Middle Ages and the emergence from them, and particularly between the eighteenth and nineteenth centuries, though appearing to be the reversal of the old principle, was in reality its dialectic development and perfection.

Before this perfection one could speak, with some reason, of a "new" or "modern" age, and the reactionary aristocrats or Catholics could point out its important characteristics and abhor it; but the socialists, who continue and want to extend that modernity, cannot degrade it by returning to an outmoded spiritual epoch, because they cannot revert to something that is analogous to that real Catholic-feudal-authoritarian-theocratic past, that which the reactionaries viewed as the ideal and criterion of judgment for the construction of their pseudohistory. The modern age recognizes socialism as one of its elements and components: even as the Jew in the drama of Bernstein recognizes in the fervent anti-Semite the son of his blood, endowed with his own impetus and his own psychology.

After this it does not seem necessary to add arguments to demonstrate the inadequacy and even nullity of the concept of the "bourgeoisie" that replaced the concept of the "modern age"; but this is an opportunity to exhort historians to guard against it as a very frequent cause of distortions and unilateral judgments in the descriptions they make and in the methods and illustrations they use. I should say that historains must

let that word become lost, leaving it to the polemics
of reactionaries and socialists, or must use it as little
as possible; that is, only in connection with certain
aspects of the past and present life to which it is appropriate, or only as a metaphor accomanied by the consciousness of its metaphorical and expressive function.

8

MANUAL WORK
AND SPIRITUAL WORK

Unhappily, it seems to me that in observing modern conditions of human society one cannot help noticing the decreased respect, if not the negligence and contempt, that is accorded spiritual work (religious, intellectual, artistic)—and consequently its diminished independence and energy—in comparison with work that is called manual and with the correlative positive science and technique that direct it. It is axiomatic that the one and the other are inseparable, interconnected in the indivisible unity of life. But the unity that is living and dialectic has in itself the moment of contrast and disharmony that historically more or less accentuates itself. And today it seems that the contrast between intellectual and manual work is more intense than ever.[1]

The possibility of contrast and disharmony is born of the distinction between work centered on the maintenance and increase of physiological life, economic or material or whatever it is known as, and work centered on the life that is considered eminently spiritual; between work that antiquity called *banausie* (low-brow work) and those that it held to be superior, admired, and (with reference to a group of them) called "beautiful"; arts that in modern times, having become synonymous with beauty, have ended up by monopolizing the name "art" for themselves alone. And since the distinctions and the dialectic of the categories of reality induce the diversity of disposition and attitudes, and since education and that which is called nature, which is also education, development, and historical formation, produce men who are disposed and particularly inclined toward the one or the other of these two forms of work, the manual and the spiritual, there are many more of the former than of the latter.

Spiritual workers constitute a minority differently attuned; but because of the aforementioned indivisible spiritual unity, theirs is a minority necessary to the majority and is its friend, and not a competitor and adversary who oppresses and exploits it—an accusation that could be imagined and believed and stated only as a result of mental infirmity or thoughtlessness. Oppressions, abuses, exploitations have occurred and still occur in history, though according to the times and places they were not always thus felt, but were resignedly accepted as necessary and legitimate, and were therefore not really the same as those that in other times and places, conditions having changed, were felt to be tyrannical and unbearable and deserving of odious epithets.

This is the "great tragedy of labor," the theme about which Antonio Labriola once eloquently outlined a sort of historical poem in which would appear, one after another, generations of workers, from ancient Egypt or Babylonia to modern England, Italy, and Germany, all of who shared the same fate and sorrow; a tragedy only in the sense that human history is always tragic. But the division of the history of workers into the three stages of slavery, serfdom, and proletariat, was not the doing of the spiritual minority; it was the product of another minority, arising out of the majority, part and parcel of the manual workers themselves, and having the same attitudes and homogeneity of intention, thought, and method, though differently directed.

The components of this different minority are above all those who were called and celebrated as the heroes and *patres,* the aristocrats and feudal barons who created and still create and govern republics and states; and here are found the industrial and commercial leaders (in a word, the men of business), to whom one owes the progress of human society in the means and circulation of wealth, and who at times are considered to be a modern aristocracy or feudality that has taken the place of the ancient one.

Even they did not come into the world to make a negative contribution, which would be a contradiction in terms, however much the times of Rousseau and the Enlightenment like to relegate them to the position already occupied by the two mythical progenitors who, eating the forbidden fruit, forfeited the earthly paradise and introduced to the world the sweat of toil. Even they play and still play a necessary and positive role, which they could not do unless they subjugated others, coercing and forcing them onward, directing and disciplining their worldly labors—in this way dominating them.

Of course they associated fatigue and risks (since they were carnal men and not saints and ascetics) with the enjoyment of comfort and wealth, which under those conditions represented the price of their daring, courage, and rendered social services; and this wage came to be considered undeserved only when they rendered no more services or when it was no longer necessary for them to render them. Any other way of interpreting the reality of these facts would be fanciful, not logical. And fanciful (as it is now known) is the economic pseudodoctrine of Marx, who views profit as unpaid labor, the value of which, at most, is as a drastic symbol of an age in which that social relationship revealed itself to be antiquated and in need of change or reform.

This historical movement has given birth to the plea expressing itself in the formula of the "emancipation of the workers"; and concerning this formula it is necessary that we understand one another clearly. Man never achieves true and proper emancipation; and when he does obtain it, he does so by himself and within himself, through his indomitable sense of liberty and moral values. Christianity, with an efficacy much greater than the ancient philosophies, announced and promoted true and proper emancipation, recognizing it in every human creature, all redeemed by the blood of Christ.

In this sense, and not in effectual economic relations that require very different and slower processes of corrosion and dissolution, Christianity not only outlawed, but abolished the very idea of slavery, and wiped away the contempt in which the Greeks and Romans held manual laborers and artisans. On the other hand, the emancipation from obstacles to our actions is only relative and particular: in the absolute sense it is not only unrealizable but undesirable, being contrary to life, because our actions and our progress have their stimulus and their substance in obstacles; this is so true that the only ones who, in their fanatic program, espouse the absolute abolition of obstacles, are the anarchists or egocentrics.

Hence the so-called emancipation of the workers (and it would be necessary to say of men in general) has importance and significance only in the particularity of history, according to the place and time, and takes place as an historical process and, as such, is characterized by the above mentioned three historical stages of its course. In the third stage the manual workers see themselves governed on a par with other men, by the same laws and, juridically made free, as participants in political or social life, and thus the shapers of their own destiny.

Not deserving of confutation, because it is so false and so base, is the odd statement that the ancient slaves were better off than the workers or modern proletarians because their masters protected them from the anxious uncertainty of today and tomorrow, providing them with food and clothing and giving them shelter, treating them, indeed, like *res* or domestic animals. But this emancipation, this ever progressive liberation from shackles offensive to the moral personality of the workers, has always found its feeling, its thoughts, its verbal expression in that minority, which here takes the primacy, of spiritual workers, the men of religion, philosophers, poets: in the men of religion who make serious utterances, challenge the rulers, and directly operate on their conscience; in the philosophers who, by stressing the common faculty of reasoning, are natural democrats and *"ab optimatibus non iniuria sibi existimati periculosi"*; (not without good

reason judged dangerous by the privileged upper class)
in the poets who, in love and sorrow, virtue and error,
admiration and pity, embrace all men, the most arrogant and the most humble, and even find piteousness
in the violent Achilles and in the criminal Macbeth
and a generous heart in the deranged Don Quixote.
They have done and still do this not by force or illusion and deceit but because of a sense of justice, truth,
and beauty; they are completely detached precisely
because they are universally concerned; nor do they
follow Utopias, the sterile Utopias outside of and opposed to reality, but rather wait for events themselves
to produce conditions that gradually bring near to
fruition the perpetual aspirations of the human soul
which in the spiritual workers are alive and efficacious.

Because of this intimate harmony and sympathy between the work of the two groups, between the majority and the minority, there is no noticeable aversion on the part of the manual workers, peasants, artisans—in the "people" as they are usually called—to
the religious apostles, the thinkers, the poets. The
humble, the oppressed, have accompanied them with
their popular religions, culturally inferior to those
from which they are derived, abundant in fable and
superstition, but nevertheless still preserving their
spirit. Let the superficial polemic of the Protestants,
for example, qualify as "paganism" the religiousness
of the Spanish and Neapolitan common people; it is
enough to point to the gentleness of the cult of the
compassionate Madonna to confirm which and how
many treasures of Christianity are contained in this
"paganism."

The spiritual leaders have been followed by the

workers with their popular literature, not really created by the workers themselves, but rather chosen,
taken up, and adapted by them as being suited to their
emotions and their mental capacity. In this literature
they evince not only their feelings of love and sorrow,
but also those of fearlessness, heroism, and bravery,
and the workers read or listen, like their rulers, with
a not dissimilar fervor and enthusiasm, to the deeds of
human courage in epics and poems of chivalry. Even
proverbs, the so-called wisdom of the people, have
been inspired by the example bequeathed by an am-
bience of reflection, thought, and knowledge. A sense
of reverence, on the part of the common people, has
surrounded the person of the learned man, the man
of knowledge who knows more than they do, though
they despair of understanding his concepts, which are
too difficult for them.

And conversely, where do the indifference, the an-
noyance, the suspicion, the hostility of the dominating,
usurping minority originate, if not exactly from the
sphere of the base or lofty interests of the powerful,
of the dominators in political and economic fields, of
those who, in particular events of historical development, assume the role of oppressors and exploiters of
other workers?

There has been not only tragedy of labor but also
"tragedy of thought" which as everyone knows, has
claimed innumerable martyrs; there has been consis-
tent persecution of spiritual men, against whom the
powerful of the earth, not satisfied with their customary devices, of war and police, have often incited the
ignorant and misled common people.

Nor is the favor they find on other occasions among

the rulers to be interpreted as a serious recognition
and as a profound awareness of the soul because, if,
in their consolidated fortunes, in their leisure, enjoy-
ments, and amusements, the rulers surround themselves with poets, artists, literary, and learned men, the
motive is the luster they confer upon their persons
and their courts. Here a communion of souls does not
occur and, even in the splendor of our courts of the
Renaissance, rare were the princes who had a sincere
love and understanding of art; and, besides, the artists,
the Ariostos, the Tassos, and numerous others, have
told us what one ought to think of the princes who
patronized them, and of their courts. While the princes
remained aloof from their intimate work, at the same
time they endeavored, as much as possible, to bend it
toward their political ends, using them as propagators
of praise and adulation. Such a condition, that the
favor of princes imposed on men of letters, moved the
generous disdain of Vittorio Alfieri [2] and impelled him
to write the treatise, *Del principe e delle lettere,* in
which he did not even forgive Virgil for allowing the
golden stream of his verse to flow in acclamation of
Augustus and his family.

With Alfieri, and lifting and fixing their eyes on the
great figure of Dante, Italian literary men started to
loosen their bond with the powerful, with the sove-
reigns and the men of business, and, jealous of their
independence from every influence other than that of
intellect and beauty, adopted a way of life in keeping
with the nobility of their office. And because among
the new influences there was, together with the liberty
to which they devoted themselves, that other and different influence related to democracy, the preference

for quantity over quality, which literary men resisted when necessary, they did not listen even to the great moral authority of a Giuseppe Mazzini, who wanted to win them over to his particular political conceptions which, highly inspired as they were, required their descent from ends to means. (Mazzini's statement, incidentally, scolding Shakespeare for being the poet of the isolated individual and not of society, I have found again on the lips of a Soviet statesman who, in my presence, scorned a creative contemporary poet for being purely "psychological" instead of being the spokesman of the proletariat.)

But the lack of reverence for spiritual work, its derogation in comparison with manual work, and the attempt to enslave it to politics, derive in our day not so much from those groups that are still called democracies, and that have lost their arrogant spirit, as from another party in which that arrogant spirit prevails, and which wants to be the rival and successor of democracy: that which is still called "communism," though it does not preserve any essential trait of the communistic ideal, being a particular nationalistic and class formation, represented certainly in the new historical age by a vast part of Europe and capable of vast undertakings.

This manifestation, however, now deserves its own, unequivocal name and not the other, which no longer fits it, or which is equivocal. Still remembered is the statement of Lenin, at the beginning of the Russian Revolution, in favor of manual work which, as opposed to intellectual work, he considered to be of sole importance; and if it seems that this original attitude may have been modified and that intellectual

work plays a more or less augmented role even in
Russia, the principle that governs it is always that of
enslavement.

In his early metaphysical improvisations, that solidified in him without any further exercise in self-criti-
cism, Marx had theorized that philosophy, art, and religion were nothing but expressions of classes and of
economic relations, and especially of capitalism, which
was the most recent manifestation and against which
he was fighting. And his modern, naive doctrinal followers, adopting as infallible this philosophical deduc-
tion and this historical interpretation, have reversed
them and have decreed that religion, poetry, and philosophy are expressions of the proletariat, that is, of
those who wage politics in its name; therefore, in
order to discipline them to this form, they do violence
to these spiritual manifestations.

The incomprehension of poetry and art, of philosophy, of moral and religious problems, and the coarse
treatment or ignorance of them have now crossed over
the Russian borders and even penetrated into our
countries of the West where, by good fortune, they
encounter other experiences, other traditions, and a
keener criticism; but despite all this, the sultry and
arid breath of incomprehension and coarseness still
makes itself felt. Even in Italy there has appeared in
profile (though it seems that it has not had the courage actually to appear on the scene) a sect of jurors or
conspiring "writers of the left," democratic or communistic, whatever they call themselves, who are disposed to serve.

And it is curious that these attempts, these ways of
thinking, these feelings usurp the aspect of "youthful

movements"; when what I have been expounding demonstrates that these are things that have a history of centuries and that have been dismissed as not being in harmony with the modern spirit of liberty and the dignity of writers. But the old people, against whom even today bold youth is invoked and incited, at least clearly perceive how long and how white, even if a little venerable, are often the beards of the so-called "ideas of the young"; and, as far as I myself am concerned, I usually repeat to myself, happily, a motto of Dumas père that strikes me as not only witty but also full of plain truth: that the young man always enters into life with an old woman at his arm and with an old idea in his brain.

9

A RECOMMENDATION
TO HISTORIANS

If I may be allowed a recommendation to our modern historians, political theorists, and publicists (a recommendation that, because of my long experience in this field is certainly not arrogant), I would say that they should remain ever watchful that their judgments and reasonings be not infiltrated by concepts derived from "historical materialism"; that they should be prompt to reject every judgment into which it has introduced itself and in which it persists.

One usually asserts that historical materialism has been confuted and surpassed, as the books on the subject and the almost total sterility of its modern literature testify, whereas the doctrine, that was so bold nearly fifty years ago, now seems to prosper (if one may speak of prosperity) only in Russia. Historical materialism has been so thoroughly refuted and surpassed that one is able to discuss it now with more detachment, trying to determine the function it fulfilled and the services it rendered, as is usually done with the facts and ideas that have become a part of the now tranquil past.

But even though one admits that the doctrine of historical materialism has been surpassed in the theoretical sphere, its superstitions or survivals, which are practically the most efficacious and insidious parts of a doctrine, remain. These vestiges survive because they operate in ignorance of their origin, without clear reference to the principle from which they proceed, and, because they are lodged in common opinion, they have the semblance of indisputable truths. Thus, they are not confined to the treatises of philosophers and scholars, but are directly connected with historical interpretations, with the judgment of political facts, with norms that are proposed for practical action.

It is necessary to keep clearly in mind the true essence of historical materialism—that is, its genesis. It is known that it was conceived, around the middle of the past century, by Marx, the philosopher of the extreme Left of Hegelianism. In that school research centered on the supreme principle, on the Absolute, by which the world is actuated. This principle, which Hegel thought of as the Logos or Idea, to which the Hegelian Right began to restore the ancient name and personality of God, and which the Left, especially the extreme Left, began to identify with Nature or Matter, was conceived by Marx—in the realm of social life, history, the only things that interested him—as Utility or Economics. Hence he prided himself on having overturned the Hegelian principle, on having replaced its head with its feet, by converting the Idea into Matter —and economic matter—which thus assumed the part of the God of old and the function of the ultimate and unique reality. All the rest of reality (thought, feeling, moral volition, science, art, religion, custom) was judged to be different from Matter only in appearance, in an illusory sense, or by the superficial intellect, yet

it was intrinsically formed of the same substance and
was thus the work, instrument, or "superstructure," as
Marx used to say, of economic activity. This explains
the ridicule Marx and his disciples heaped upon morality, speculation, poetry, elevation toward the divine,
likening them to pretenders who, though they believed
in their own reality, were no more than shadows. Marx
replaced the notorious Hegelian "panlogism" with a
paradoxical "paneconomism."

And this constituted the most radical opposition to
the liberal-political conception that had been formed,
with the steady improvement of the spiritual life of
humanity throughout antiquity, Christianity, the Renaissance, the religious Reformation—these were movements which, at the center of history, placed conscience and moral ideality as the sole movers of every
manifestation of goodness and truth, which alone govern and direct the economic process itself. And those
liberal writers who thought to accept the Marxian theories or to absorb some elements, almost, as it were, to
correct and to integrate what in their ideology seemed
too idealistic or too generic or too abstract, were not
fully aware that such a compromise ended only in con-
tamination, there being doctrines whose animating
principles are repugnant to each other. Shortcomings,
if any, noted in the liberal theories, had to be cor-
rected by understanding and developing in a more
profound and concrete manner their principle itself,
and not by turning for help to a principle that was
not only different but calculated to strike down and
destroy the other at its vital center.

As we have said, philosophical criticism has corroded historical materialism in its every aspect, again

finding in it (just because it was the overturned Hegelianism) the same error and evil consequences of Hegelian panlogism, which fails to recognize, and compromises, the originality and autonomy of the various spiritual manifestations which, in their distinction and unity, are the very process of the human spirit, its creative liberty. And against Marxism criticism has vindicated, as it did against Hegelianism, the respective manifestations denied by the one or the other: against Hegel, creative imagination and practical activity; against Marx, morality, creative imagination, and thought. Moreover, criticism has demonstrated the disharmony of the Marxian principle, which was economics—that is, man's activity—and, as such, also spiritual activity; instead, this activity of man revealed itself as "Matter"; therefore materialism, which was antihistorical in essence, presented itself as "historical materialism."

However, from the economic point of view the great distortion, perpetrated by Marx and his school, of the concepts of social and political theory, and of history, has left its no less clear imprints everywhere; and these imprints are maintained and continuously restored, not only generically by the vulgar, shrewd, and false acumen, always ready to suspect everywhere financial ambition and secondary ends, but also by those impetuously economic tendencies of contemporary society. In effect, the working class, on account of its particular interests, psychology, and the theories that are administered to it, is induced to give first—rather, the unique—place, for the explanation of facts, for practical ideals, for its programs and methods of action, to the economic principle.

The same disposition shows itself in the capitalistic and plutocratic class which defends itself against the working class with weapons of the same temper; and in some countries it has even copied the methods and institutions of the proletarian dictatorship, attempting to put them at the service of the capitalistic-pluto-cratic dictatorships or eclectic combinations of differ-ent competitive interests. This has caused more than one observer to assert that the liberal spirit has been extinguished and that at the same time the ethical ideality and political art, which were an integral part of it, have come to an end; that the present and the foreseeable future will belong entirely to economics.

I have no desire to show disrespect toward the pluto-crats and the proletarians, the industrialists and the workers; but I do not believe that I do them an injus-tice by reminding them that both groups fulfill every function except that of the care of souls—that is, in-terest in moral and political life and in the education of human societies. Since they concentrate on work and on the production of wealth, are completely ab-sorbed in it, are little sensitive to other, spiritual in-terests, are deprived of and scarcely curious about the correlative culture, they are not in a position to un-derstand correctly the essence of those problems; and usually when they discuss them it is in such a way as to bring a smile to the lips of the specialists who, in the great managers of wealth, frequently see over-grown children or men of childlike innocence.

If some of these industrialists and workers arrive at an understanding of those problems, they actually ac-quire a consciousness superior to their profession or trade, and with this they really bring not contrary proof but confirmation of what has just been said. As far as those things are concerned, humanity has always entrusted their care to "spiritual people"—the founders and reformers of religion, the apostles and priests, and then the men of intellect and knowledge and those who, impelled by a profound political passion, become the arm and sword of ideas: kings, captains, ministers, revolutionaries, men of action.

The spiritual leaders' renunciation of the leadership of society in favor of the workers or industrialists, or of a combination of both, would not redound to the benefit of the workers or the industrialists but rather to the advantage of those spiritual leaders who are characterized by a deteriorating spirituality—the rhetoricians and demagogues, flatterers and adventurers of the pen. Such men would provide the workers and industrialists with those ideas and those words that otherwise workers and industrialists lack since they only know the concepts and the words of work and wealth. The thinkers and writers who now resignedly give assurance that the future government of societies will not be ethical-political but economic, and who with this assertion withdraw and surrender, become guilty of an illicit modesty and humility, like he who abandons a right that is also a duty.

Meanwhile these thinkers and writers, in order effectively to restore the depressed consciousness of liberty and, as I was saying, in order to hunt down all those survivals of the Marxian concepts that confuse modern doctrines and political discussions, would do better if they took seriously the confutation of historical materialism made by the philosophers.

Let us take an example: the concept of the "ruling

class" interpreted in an economic sense. Modern historiography, even that which is not socialistic, is full
of this concept; and in order to explain actions and
political events this historiography views as a ruling
class now that of the landowners, now that of the industrialists, now that of the bankers, now that of the
petite bourgeoisie, now that of the urban workers or
peasants. But in reality none of these classes, as such,
had ruled, and none can ever rule, because there is a
true and proper difference between the care or the
protection of particular economic interests and the
government of society. In this governing function it is
required that economic factors be reduced to a simple
matter of government, and that over and above them
there should be a governmental aim that will always
be an ethical ideal, more lofty or more base, more cultivated or more coarse, but an ideal and not an economic interest. Even in the worst moments of history,
even in the most troubled or badly governed states,
this ideal comes to the surface and lives. The true ruling political class is the ruling class with religious,
philosophical, moral concepts, whatever they may be.

I suggest that we look at what is now happening to
the studies, dear to Italians and others, of the history
of Florence from the thirteenth to the fifteenth century: a history which seemed to be typical of the history of politics as an alternate or successive rule of
classes and fractions of economic classes. By going
deeply into the subject, it has finally been discovered
that the policy of the Florentine Republic, and its correlative revolutions, was initiated and carried forward
not by the economic classes, that is, by the major and

minor arts, but by the "general" or political class that always went beyond those partial interests.

Let us take another example: the "class struggle," which plays such an important role in modern historiography whose disposition is to accept the Marxian aphorism "every history is the history of the struggle of classes." Parenthetically, this definition entailed the strange consequence that, because communism would terminate the class struggle, it would also put an end to human history! However, it is certain that the classes and all economic groups (groups more numerous than the two classes, of capitalists and workers, of simple Marxian reduction), because they differ among themselves, though at times they form mutual alliances and harmoniously work together for the common good, enter into conflicts and struggles.

These diversities and these agreements are in themselves the material substance and not the creative spirit of history, which is the struggle not for economic advantages but of ethical ideals, not of "classes" but of political "parties." Historiography, which was anterior to that of historical materialism and which explained human events in the light of ideas (religious Reformation and Catholic counter-Reformation, criticism and authority, *natural laws* and traditionalism, Historicism and Jacobinism, etc.), grasped the essential truth. Hegel was more profound than his materialistic or "economic" disciple, and Leopold Ranke was a better historian than Karl Marx.

And here is a third example: the "bourgeoisie." What has become of the great movement of modern civilization which, at the end of the Middle Ages, con-

tinued the tradition of classic culture; formed a new
conception of the world; founded the science of nature; created a poetry and art encompassing Dante
and Michelangelo, Shakespeare and Goethe; produced
new state structures, from the absolute and enlight-
ened monarchies to the parliamentary regimes; performed prodigies of technique and work through
science?

Under the influence of the *Communist Manifesto,*
in modern historiography such toil has been assumed
by the "bourgeoisie"—that is, by the capitalists and industrialists (an economic class), and therefore it has
been intimately connected with the economy of that
class: a class that the proletariat (a new economic
class) threatens to overthrow and to replace. But that
toil is, instead, the harmonic-disharmonic work of the
whole of humanity, of pure humanity, which always
works as a whole, always grows and never dies, and
hands down its work and its dreams to future generations. This work is immortal, and future generations
will continue it, not as an economic, or not exclusively
economic, enterprise, but in the variety of its spiritual
forms, as work that is the fruit of the spirit in its
oneness.

The concept of the "bourgeoisie," understood as a
concept of spiritual totality, falsifying this totality or
contaminating it with extraneous elements, must be
expunged from modern historiography and confined
to its strictly economic meaning of a class that pre-
pares and manages the instruments of work, just as in
medieval history (and in that of the ancien régime)
the concept of the bourgeoisie had an essentially juridical meaning.

And here I must stop. But I feel the urge to add that the consequences of such residues of historical materialism, irrationally accepted or thoughtlessly tolerated, also show themselves to have serious practical consequences, as may be seen, among other things, in the dictum that the socialists have coined and that many nonsocialists accept or let pass: "liberty" is a "bourgeois concept." Hence the ulterior consequence that proletarian society and the industrial one, extreme democracy and extreme aristocracy, can and must do without that elementary exigency of the spirit and of reality.

But this liberty is not an aspect of the bourgeoisie or any other economy, but of the human soul and its profound needs; it has not an economic origin or quality but a moral and religious one; it is, in a word, the modern form of Christianity. And Christianity—here Hegel was right—must be considered as the "absolute religion," as the religion that can always be further developed and continuously elaborated and strengthened, but that can never be wrested from the heart of man.

10

THE MONOTONY AND EMPTINESS
OF COMMUNIST HISTORIOGRAPHY

Communist historiography is monotonous, empty, and
tedious. But this monotony and tedium disappear
when one lifts one's eyes toward another multifarious
historiography, a historiography that is highly colored
with our cultural and our human life, that is passionate, extremely moving, and intricately connected
through many threads with the aspects and thoughts
of reality. But communist historians condemn and de-
spise every historiography other than their own, and
call them "bourgeois" and "vulgar" precisely because
of the existence of the historiography of Karl Marx.

This historiography, with a power which might be
described as historical-radioscopic, made transparent
the skeleton, the economic structure underlying the
whole edifice of history. Through this concept communist historiography interpreted with self-assurance
not only European history of the last two centuries but
also world-wide history, because the substance of both
is always the same: the undeserved exploitation that
until now the ruling minorities have perpetrated on
the people. And, after the astonishment at this great
discovery, a pious concern was manifested toward
Marx's scattered and partial precursors. Among them

one must recall Saint-Simon, the first to define the
class character of the French Revolution; and the sur-
viving friend of Babeuf, Filippo Buonarroti, who in
that revolution saw the collision of two systems, the
"system of selfishness or private property" and the
"system of social equality," or communism. Buonarroti also saw the victory of the former over the latter
in the destruction of Robespierre and in the cessation
of the healthy system of the Terror.

Even in Italy one has witnessed the emergence of
communist historians who reject all the existing interpretations of the national Risorgimento and plan to
write another new scientific history in the light of the
economic and materialistic criterion. These historians
find their precursor in Carlo Pisacane [1] who, in the
undertaking of Sapri, encountered death and glory.
But he deserves, according to these historians, another
glory in another field for having initiated in 1850 a
much desired historical treatment: a treatment he had
learned from contemporary French socialism and
communism.

The Italian intellectuals and professors, who have
become recent converts to the new religion, take pains
in this task of reevaluation. And among these professors and intellectuals there are some who, alternating
timidity with courage, would like to obey the instruc-
tions of the party and to satisfy its desires by applying
the same materialistic method to the history of our
poetry. But in this respect one should charitably advise
the eager communists to go slowly, because Italians do
not easily adjust themselves to the mistreatment and
distortion of artistic genius.

However these distorted judgments and these ex-

travagant claims may fail to convince me, there is a
point of theoretical and critical character that arouses
my curiosity. How is it possible—I ask myself—that
communism can consider itself capable of writing history when it is the absolute negation of history?

History is the story of struggles, and communism
does not recognize any struggle except that of putting
an end once and for all, by means of its own violent
action, to all struggles; and therefore it intends to
fight assiduously their causes and creators. The communist ideal is peace among men; and because the
communists believe that the struggle is born of the
work of evil against good, they infer that the way to
strip the world of struggle is to strip it of evil. Communists investigate this problem and conclude that
the cause of evil is private property, with its accom-
panying institutions, and therefore that the removal
of private property, which is considered the evil of
evils or the source of all others, is the solution. Once
this removal is effected, a doubt will arise: whether
history, which is the history of struggles (and these
feed themselves on evil), can continue. In this way the
epoch that will begin after the end of struggles will
not be a true epoch (a differentiated halting-place in
the world of history) because it will, rather, present the
character of that epoch called eternity. But this doubt
that we experience never occurs to those ardent destroyers of the struggle among men and restorers of
perpetual peace, and in every case the destroyers could
proudly answer: *Fiat iustitia et pereat mundus* (let
there be justice and let the world perish), in spite of
Hegel's wise correction of the saying—*ne pereat mundus* (so that the world may not perish).

Consequently, this reasoning is very superficial, or rather, extremely superficial. But really the evil lies (conceding the play on words) exactly in that concept of evil that has great surprises in store for anyone who cares to meditate upon it seriously. And, in order to meditate upon it, one must start with those aspects of our soul that we fight in every act and every moment of our lives and that we view as evils.

Evil would be, for example, an act that I have committed under the impulse of passion and whose quality and consequences I have not scrutinized. Therefore at first I have not felt nor judged this act as evil until the moment in which the act appears to me in a new aspect and gives me that form of sorrow which is called remorse and which arouses my desire to erase the evil in the only possible way: to see to it that the act is succeeded by another and different one.

In this process of remorse and inward effort I finally arrive at the new liberating act, which gives me peace. By now, having acquired this calm, and beholding what was grieving and tormenting me as evil, I view it with different eyes. I consider that the whole thing was not entirely evil but that it had some good in itself because, without it, I would never have arrived at this new world of good, in which I find myself more firm and secure. This security is the outcome of the fact that I have become aware of the unreflective impetuousness that was lurking within me and that led me to an act which, at that instant, seemed to me to be necessary and reasonable.

Is the act, then, not completely evil? How can an effective act be both evil and good, that is, contradictory, and because of this contradiction, unrealizable?

Therefore one must decide, and, in homage to logic and truth, say that that act was good but that it appeared—and must necessarily appear—to me as evil, in the light of the new act to be performed and because of the effort that it cost and must cost me in order to achieve spiritual separation from the previous act for the realization of the new one.

The same process takes place in the realization of truth. At times we are satisfied with a doctrine we have formulated or received. But later this doctrine is corroded by doubt, and because of this doubt we enter into a painful situation, like that of someone who gropes in darkness. In this painful situation we are not capable even of exposing as false what we had first accepted, because in order to affirm this negation a new criterion or doctrine is necessary: a doctrine we still do not have. However, when finally we come to possess the new doctrine, the first doctrine (if it was an act of thought and not a vain *flatus vocis* [sound of voice] or fanciful intoxication) shows itself to be true also; but it is to be integated into this new truth. Consequently we possess a union of the two doctrines, a unification that gives them vigor.

The conclusion is that evil, when it is a reality, is not evil, but that when evil is evil it is not a reality—a conclusion that does not exclude the fact that moral conscience has as its own instrument this ghost of the irrational and evil; that here assuredly the true law of moral conscience retrospectively produces "sin," and exercises its supreme right to operate in such a way that reality may not lose its substance by remaining statically inert and by annulling itself, but that it may develop from and grow out of itself.

What is true for man as an individual is also true for social man or human society, in which particular spiritual forces are personified by men who struggle among themselves, each of them sometimes an enemy and sometimes a friend, sometimes a conquered being, sometimes a conqueror. This is human history that stretches to the infinite because, if the series were to end in the finite, this would happen: the world would cease to exist. Hence it appears evident that communist ideology, in regard to the struggle between evil and good, has been formulated without its having defined either the struggle or the evil, playing these terms by ear.

Also played by ear is the concept of private property and of its abolition, because private property will never be abolished completely, insofar as it coincides with the concept of the individual. The individual does not live as a class or other generality but with himself and with whatever enables him to exist.

However, private property can be modified in its forms and proportions. And it has been so modified many times in history. Property has not always been private, but at times public, governmental, and communal; and perhaps it would be possible to augment that of the latter. The problem of solving how much one can amplify the communal or governmental aspect without diminishing, but rather increasing, the production of resources for sustaining life, is a problem that is contingent. That is, it depends on place and time. The modifications of property are relative to particular circumstances, and they sometimes require increased, sometimes reduced, governmental activity. In this sphere, experience is the only teacher.

The highly significant character of communism, and
the clear confirmation of its conscious or unconscious
negation of history, are the perpetual aversion and repugnance toward a fundamental concept of the life of
the spirit and history: the concept of "liberty." This
concept failed to find a place in the old Utopias of the
type of the *City of the Sun*,[2] just as it does in the modern communist parties, which try to realize themselves
by practical and political means.

The concept of "liberty" is opposed by the already
mentioned "Society of Equals" of Babeuf, who up-
holds the idea of a "real" liberty that complements
"formal" liberty: a living proof of the misunderstand-
ing of the concept of liberty which is always "formal,"
that is, "moral,' and that is never conditioned by the
possession of particular economic goods.

The concept of "liberty" is also opposed by the
theories of Marx, who always ridiculed it, except
when he was encouraging the efforts of the liberals
against absolute regimes, with the firm intention of
ridding himself of these occasional allies and of at-
taining on his own the passage from the "Kingdom of
Necessity to the Kingdom of Liberty." The meaning
of this latter phrase is obscure, but we know that
Marx's entrance door was "temporary dictatorship,"
which would effect the "abolition of the state"—that
is, of the first juridical institution as the guarantee of
liberty.

Another solemn confirmation of the negation of history is Marx's irreverence toward all manifestations of
spiritual life, such as religion, philosophy, science,
poetry—irreverence and disesteem that had already
displayed themselves in the beginnings of modern

communism, as with the above-mentioned Babeuf. Babeuf's first Manifesto of the Society of Equals proclaimed that the "value of intelligence is a matter of opinion"; that one needs to examine "whether the value of the strength of the whole natural and physical being is not worth as much as intelligence."

The Manifesto went further: "The intellectuals themselves are the ones who have put such great value on the concepts of the brain." Finally, Babeuf aroused conflict among the authors of the Manifesto when he included a statement that seemed imprudent to some of them: "If it is necessary, let all the arts perish as long as effective equality remains."

Marx went even further; he denied the autonomous value of those manifestations, theorizing that they were nothing but masks or "superstructures" of the class struggle, leaving for him only one true manifestation: economics.

But in Marx economics, because it was isolated and unrelated to the other manifestations, was reduced from a spiritual form to a material entity, and he called his doctrine "materialism": a materialism in which religion, philosophy, art, science, morality, and their correlative histories, were unthinkable. And the history of millenniums, that "universal history," presents men's sorrows intertwined with their love, the misfortunes with the glories, the sufferings with the creations of high culture, scientific discoveries, beautiful works of art, the actions of heroes, and the sacrifice of martyrs. In Marx, this "universal history" becomes a history of the continuous oppression of the people, of miseries and horrors, the only hope being for an apocalyptic millennium.

I have always felt and still feel repugnance toward the naturalistic and fatalistic doctrine of the races. But in this instance I cannot help thinking, not about Marx's racial blood, but about the Jewish traditions and habits of Marx and about what the Romans saw in the singular historical formation of the Jewish people (*adversus omnes alios hostile odium*) (a hostile dislike of all others). In Marx, all of this results in hatred toward the whole of human history—of classical times, of the Christian Middle Ages, of modern liberty—and these cultural phenomena, instead of being represented by Homer, Dante, Shakespeare, Plato, Kant, and Hegel, are represented by Slave, Serf and Proletariat.

This Jewish vision of history is connected with what Goethe noted in his *Wanderjare* in regard to the Jews: they cannot blend with us because they do not recognize, he said, the historical origins of our culture, but rather find repugnant our history that is not their history: a history characterized by their singular idea of domination.

But, regardless of this psychological problem and its given solution, there remains in Marx the error of history conceived as evil and of the reduction of the whole of spiritual life to a mask of evil. The ultimate root of the communist ideal, an ideal not to be found in the active spiritual and moral life of men, is easily seen in the vain and puerile desire for liberation from fatigue and sorrow, which are inseparable from life and from the mainsprings of life.

Insofar as its origin may thus be located, the communist ideal has nothing to do with its expressed desire for a "better humanity," a desire that is always alive in men and that actualizes itself in the particularity of their actions and advances. Here, instead, the desire for a better humanity is understood in the sense of a humanity essentially different from our humanity, of a world different from the world that we know. This is the myth of the "above," of the "other world," Elysium, Eden, Paradise, Kingdom of the Elect, etc. Certainly, in the myth there is always a mixture of fancy and a certain amount of truth, though the latter is not expressed in philosophical form. In this case the truth consists of the concept of immortal life, in which the spirit is free from the body, does not feel and does not suffer with the body, has achieved peace and repose, but nevertheless acts operosely and participates in the reality of human work that eternizes itself beyond the life of the individual.

We can clarify this further. The truth consists of the concept of immortal life in which the spirit participates through the historical process (which continues beyond the life of the individual), through the efficacious immortality not only of all those who are famous but also of all those whose names are forgotten, yet whose deeds and function still live on in our world. And the purpose for which man creates his works— *nos, non nobis*—is to (we [create], but not for ourselves) make them so beautiful that they may separate themselves from his transient personality and live in a superior realm, not outside but within life itself.

In any case, it happens that the myth is materialized, and what first had been placed outside the world is brought back into it, and, instead of being recognized as the ideality, of which I have spoken above, the myth is recognized as having a particular purpose to be realized on earth.

This is another way, though a longer one, of realizing the communist ideal. Marx not only took this road, already opened by religions, but also added another religious myth: the myth of the lost paradise that must be regained. For him, this religious myth became the myth of primitive communism that had been lost in the course of history and whose loss was expiated through a gradual sequel of punishments; that is, the three ages, of slavery, serfdom, and proletariat: ages that will disappear when this primitive communism is regained through the rational establishment or self-awareness of communism.

Through our analysis of these concepts, we can conclude that the logical emptiness of the communist idea does not need, nor is it possible for it to find, justification in historical narration; rather, our analysis helps historical narration to explain why the communist ideal has never been realized. The communist ideal, that was the object of idyllic fancy in the old books of communist Utopias, was soon belied when it attempted to realize itself through the foundation of colonies—small colonies of believers and enthusiasts who, living a difficult life, soon died out.

For a long time Marx waited for the revolutionary catastrophe of bourgeois society. He predicted its coming from one decade to another, and he thought that it would coincide with a crisis in world economy. He believed that this crisis would be similar to that of the years 1846–47, that had given birth, according to him, to the year 1848, and to its great hopes that were frustrated when the crisis ended. But these general crises, that he believed to be the necessary consequences and fatal effects of the capitalist structure, did not repeat themselves, and at about that time Jevons in his conclusion attributed the cause to sunspots!

However that may be, none of the great states has ever had a communist revolution; nor is there an exception in the case of modern Russia and of the states and territories occupied by its armies as a result of the war. Russia is communist only in appearance, as everyone knows—everyone who has eyes to see and ears to hear. And everyone also knows that the communism and doctrines of Marx, to which the Russian politicians resort, are simply instruments of political propaganda in the hands of Russia.

A German writer, who traveled through that country in the first years of the Bolshevik regime, amazed at not seeing in its institutions the realization of communism and having his questions answered by the assertion that whatever was lacking would come into being later, observed with a smile that, as regards this at least, in Russia the verb is always conjugated in the future.

The quality of the political regime that has been shaped there and that bears the name of communism does not abolish the state, as Marx prescribed; rather, communism has established such a strong and absolute state as has never been seen in the past, not even under czarism, which was not "totalitarian" and which never reached the modern perfection of totalitarianism. Communism has not achieved economic equality, and the range of salaries between the workers and the upper ranks is considerable; strikes are not allowed, and the peasant is tied to the soil and the worker to his factory. Communism has not succeeded in giving birth to a new philosophy, a new art, religion, or mo-

rality—which today have the same meaning as these
designations imply, and which, at the same time, are
materialistic and proletarian doctrines. But communism has succeeded in depressing spiritual life in all
its manifestations, even though it is not possible to
tear out the hidden embryos of these manifestations:
manifestations that will be born again in the same
way as in the primitive and savage era.

The nullity of communist historiography cannot be
compared with that which is called "tendentious," and
which is justly rebuked for the alterations it intro-
duces into the world of truth, and which has as its
purpose the achieving of oratorical effects and prede-
terminate practical actions. But the blemishes of this
historiography are only partial falsifications—not a
total falsification of history which, for its own purposes, it tries to respect as far as possible. Communist
historiography, denying the genuine idea of life itself
and replacing it with the dualism, be it Parsiism or
Manicheism, of the struggle of evil against good, of
the good that is equality against the evil that is inequality, ends with the final triumph of equality,
which will abolish inequality and thus abolish history.
Therefore this historiography is a total falsification
and nothingness.

Historiography has as its fundamental character
what is commonly called "objectivity" and "impartiality" and denies those facts of a negative nature that
constitute contradictions in terms. This historiography
views all facts as positive, recognizes the rationality of
each, or rather the function of each fact in the historical process as seen by the historian, and with this the

reciprocity of the bond with other facts which this reciprocity equalizes and dignifies.

The historian is like a physician who diagnoses a disease to the extent that he perceives it, not as a thing extraneous to nature but as a natural process among all other natural processes. And historical consciousness is so firm in this conviction, so sure of itself and of the impossibility of falling short of its own nature and essence that, in conformity with the unselfish nature of true historical research, which can be expressed by the saying, *omnia munda mundis* (to the pure all things are pure), it has no qualms about admitting into its company the practical tendencies (political polemics, recommendations, et cetera) of historians that, regardless of explicit philosophical views, are easily found in all historical writings.

On the other hand, this has been viewed as proof that an impartial historical narration is not possible and has never been achieved; and this has led to the belief that impartiality is only possible in the indifference of the chronicle or in pure philologism. However, it is necessary to say that a book of history is not exclusively "historical thought" and that, because it is crystallized by word and style, it exhibits the personality of the writer, who, though he be historian or philosopher, cannot leave his personality at the threshold if it is to speak again in the quality of his words.[3]

But the historian, in taking his practical and morally engaged self with him, does not confuse; rather he makes clearly evident the distinction between the thinker and the man of passions; and so one can say that the historian reminds the integrated man that every historical thought must end in moral duty and personal action. This is the reason why every book of history contains an element of oratory, recommendation, political polemic, and it would be a bad sign were it to lack passion for subject matter that is the essence of history: a passion that sharpens the historian's own intelligence, while a tepid attitude and indifference tend to mislead it, as we have pointed out, toward mere chronicle and philologism. To what extent one element must contain itself with regard to the other, the intellective toward the passionate, is a problem that literary taste—which is also called common sense—solves case by case.

But the nullity of communist historiography is sealed by the fact that communism, being incapable of any historiography, cannot write, that is, *think,* even in terms of its own history; and it would be without history if nonpartisan or impartial historiography, in its liberal outlook on life, did not concern itself with the philosophical and critical examination which certainly cannot neglect a group of facts as conspicuous as those that, during the last century, have gone under the name of communism. But, in dealing with communism, philosophical historiography will illuminate it differently from the way in which pseudohistoriography does, or the way the historically biased communist invective represents itself, because, above all, communism's mental genesis is not directly found in the sufferings and agitations of the working masses. Its genesis is found in the thought that has projected (as did not occur either with the revolt of the slaves and gladiators of antiquity, or with the *jacqueries* and wars of peasants of later times) those movements and social upheavals toward problems, or in the men of culture and in the moral, liberal, and Christian conscience, that infused those problems with its own solicitude; and in the political class that began to translate them into practical measures.

Hence the fact, extraneous in appearance but obvious in reality, that all the promoters of communism and socialism belonged to that class which the factious polemic abhors and despises and calls "bourgeois." [4] And certainly the first measures in defense of workers and in the assertion of their rights were enacted by the parliaments which, beginning with the great English inquiries into working conditions, initiated the social legislation that has developed more and more during the past century.

In the first half of the nineteenth century the term "social question" was born and came to be considered the great "question of the century." This term, though it aroused the vivacious denial of a politician such as Gambetta (whose notorious saying, *la question sociale n'existe pas,* is found in a letter of Flaubert in the year 1857), was certainly not valid in the Utopian expectations it carried within itself, but in the facts to which it referred. These facts were the new physiognomy of modern industry and its related working class, the feeling that resulted from the supreme gravity of the emerging contrasts and conflicts, and the necessity to regulate them so that the tree should not be cut down in order to gather the fruit.

But the active and patient work of the governments was suspected, discredited, and criticized by the communists because they intended to cut and not just loosen the knot or knots, and by violence realize com-

pletely their ideal and make the transition or leap
from the existent society to an entirely new one.
Therefore they preferred the worsening of social conditions that, stimulating revolt, gave hope of starting
a revolutionary movement. Nevertheless, with its negation and threats, communism operated in a somewhat
positive way by disposing reluctant men and classes to
yield to the necessities of the times because generous
enthusiasm, those "nights of the fourth of August,"
which are weak and rare manifestations, could not be
counted on. Other manifestations or social effects of
communism are less praiseworthy and less beneficial:
such as "class hatred," which was not spontaneously
felt but was aroused in the souls of the proletarian
classes through the easy alliance of the minor, healthy
feelings of greed and envy; such as the diminution of
the previously recognized position of culture and the
substitution by crude propaganda that permits, and
moreover poisons, ignorance; or such as the scarcely
respectful treatment of the proletarian classes themselves, described as the "masses," of which the demagogues avail themselves and which they regard as human tools for their fanaticism or ambition, but which
they neither know, nor love, as they were known, understood, and loved by the artists of the past. (Nor are
the masses understood or loved by the artists of the
party, because those artists are deprived of this gift or
lose it in assuming such a function. And of no use are
the recent Russian schools of proletarian art, which are
as little fruitful to art as to the proletariat.)

However, these useless and harmful things were not
such as to cause great apprehension about the fate of
human society, because ignorance is sterile and its

roots are weak. What has caused the new advance of communism has not been its ideal and social force, but the great wars of the twentieth century, that have effected the destruction, or rather the suicide, of the powerful, industrious, and flourishing Germany, and the division of Europe (and one can say of the world) into two powers. One, in its liberal and historical complexity, is the West, and the other, antihistorical and dictatorial, is the East, led by Russia. This latter power, which as every power, has an imperialistic tendency, could certainly not give up, in the realm of politics and war, a quick and effective means of domination and restrain itself from planting the flag of communism and Marxism in other territories; or from causing discord and debilitation among its adversaries.

Through these means communism has developed a strength it did not have before the two wars, when it was languishing everywhere. Now, it is one of the major forces in the world; though, in achieving this high degree of strength, it has dissolved altogether as communism, has shown the unreality of its ideal, and has become simply "Slavism"—that is, the mask of that Slavic threat that appeared on the European and world scene soon after the victory won by Russia over Napoleon.

After experiencing many vicissitudes in the course of a century, and after almost disappearing and even being forgotten, that Slavic threat has finally been revivified and magnified through the fall of czarism and the dissolution of the generous but skeptical, fanciful, and lazy, nobility that surrounded it. And through the advent of a new czarism it has realized a social revolution formed and supported by unscrupulous hierarchies which, armed with modern techniques, are only concerned with the will to power.

As in Russia, so in the minds of the communists who constitute large parties in other countries. There is nothing left of the once rationalistic and humanitarian communism, but only the bewitchment of the Slavic imperialism by which they are captivated and which they communicate to others as the almost imminent fate of Europe and the world. Thus, although the communists continue to recite the Marxist catechism, it is observed that the more insistently it is recited, so much less is it believed and so much less is it felt in science and culture, which actually advance without it, though they are annoyed by the clamor of its stentorian voice.

Communist historiography now presents itself as the historiography of good against evil, of communist, humanitarian, and peace-loving Russia against the capitalist Western world which has the inhuman heart of the usurer and is pitilessly eager for new wars and new bloodshed. I do not dare assert that there are those, accustomed to criticism and to probing their innermost depths, who believe in this new mythology of light and darkness; but certainly there are many people who persuade themselves into believing in it. This thing saddens those of us who do not care to live during times in which there abound spiritual uncouthness, the blurring of the distinction between the lie and the truth; when attention is centered on one's own comfort and one's own fear, and the soul has hardened to such an extent that it seems to be confronted not by men like us but by mechanically built automata, which have a strong logical coherence, and with which one does not have any communion of thought or affection; and when all mutual understanding is precluded.

But among the shadows of this pessimism the vision of the vast numbers who suffer the same sadness returns. And, gathering to ourselves this fraternity of sorrow, our determination strengthens, to defend the heritage we have received from the spirits who created, with the work of centuries, this unique civilization conceived as a perpetual amplification and enrichment of itself, and whose destiny is momentarily entrusted to us.

11

THE HISTORY OF COMMUNISM AS
A POLITICAL REALITY

About a half century ago a group of the most eminent
socialist and Marxian writers, under the direction of
Bernstein and Kautsky, began to write a history of socialism and communism on the pattern of the universal and national histories that were being written by
bourgeois scholars—that is, by collaborating specialists. When the first volume came out,[1] I was making
my first scholarly efforts, and in one of my essays I ob-
jected to that history, because it lacked development,
"was not a history; rather it was a sort of anthology of
all the rebellions of the proletarians and of all the social theories which more or less had as their foundation the common ownership of goods." [2]

At that time I was in my youth and, as such, full of
a certain youthful radicalism and political naïveté;
and since I was experiencing my first encounter with
the intoxicating thought of Marx, I could not really
fathom the essence of communism. Had I been more
mature, I should have denied that communism, as
such, gives birth to history; that communism has the
capacity of being the subject of history.

Indeed the subject of history is the positive and not
the negative; and the nucleus of communism, in its ul-

timate and governing idea, in the principle that it espouses, is not the positiveness of an action or an institution, but a movement toward a void. It is an effort which, in its clearest expression, views the ideal or perfect life as peace without contrasts and competition, and which looks upon all the components of society as having equal feelings and concepts, equal and satisfied needs.

Were this view true, it would destroy the necessity for, and the very possibility of the struggles of some groups or classes against others, of the victories and defeats of those upper and lower classes, and the necessity for the state organization itself. Every theoretical error has a stimulus or practical stimulation, and in this case the stimulus is to be found in the fear of the travail and sorrow of the life struggle, that one tries to avoid by dreaming of a life without struggle; in other words, a life without life.

Therefore communism, in its fundamental idea, is not only a utopia; it is an absolute, irredeemable, unrealizable utopia in whatever age, be it the most futuristic or most recent one. Some ages have appeared to be the historical realization of this Utopia, as is evident in certain religious sects that founded small colonies, or, according to some communist historians, in the Jesuit missions of Paraguay, the monasteries, and other similar institutions of the churches. But such historians neglect the fact that these historical realizations very soon degenerated, decayed, or dissolved, and that they did not stand on their own feet but were parts of a noncommunist society, of which they were parasitic formations or instruments and delegations with certain specific purposes.

Communism does not even succeed in creating the historical manifestations of this Utopia in the world of fancy unless it reduces men to puppets, devoid of nerves and blood, imagination, thought, and will. Stranger still, as one observes the naive creation of ideal or model cities in ancient times, is the fact that communism is peculiarly reserved for the aristocratic and governing classes, as in Plato; or for the aristocrats who rule over slaves, as in Thomas More. It is a sort of "lordly freedom," according to Vico—that is, a "lordly communism."

The liberal conception of life and history is not the antithesis of the communist thesis, nor the adversary it fights on the same plane. Were the liberal conception the antithesis, it would give the communist conception a philosophical quality it does not deserve and would lower itself by preparing and predicting the outdistancing, of both liberalism and communism, by a third undiscoverable and ineffable form. The relationship between the liberal and communist conceptions is the relationship between one who has greater experience and meditative powers and one who has less experience and is therefore involved in misunderstandings and equivocations, or is given to fancy. And the liberal conception appreciates that life is a becoming, and therefore perpetual contrast and perpetual solution, perpetual solution and perpetual newborn contrast, continuous newborn inequality and agitation, and destruction of peace and welfare. Peace and destruction of peace do not constitute the purpose of life, because the purpose of life is life itself in its fullness, whose sacred, mysterious being one must worship, not desecrate, nor pretend to correct by tampering with and breaking the source of action itself—that is, life.

The liberal conception, however, also recognizes that man can and always does transfer the vital contrast to a higher plane; and this is the faith that molds its action; this is what is called perpetual progress, advancement, enrichment, and refinement of human life. One who knows does not overlook or treat with indifference and ridicule the errors of one who does not know, but becomes aware of the motivations of these errors and, attributing them to difficulties, anxieties, and human desires, tries to remove them.

So the liberal mind becomes pensive before the assertions and the demands of communism and, though it sees the evident contradiction of the communist principle of solution, and fights the errors of communist assertions, that forever take new forms, it always endeavors to satisfy communism's practical ends, in accordance with their own particularities, when the means to realize them are found or when these means and conditions are being formed.

The liberal mind endeavors to satisfy communism's practical demands as long as they are deeply thought decisions and the consequences, not of communism's premises or conditions, but of mental and moral liberty. On its part the liberal order gives man whatever it should give: freedom of speech and the press, association, propaganda, elections, representations, plebiscite, the rights of the majority.

Liberal men, if they really understand, must make use of these means in order to try to persuade others in the political and economic worlds and in order to gather forces which adhere to their purposes. But let

not these forces ask liberal men to use force and violence in order to satisfy their desires. This is not to
say that the liberal soul absolutely rejects so-called revolutions, suspension of legality, and interruptions of
the regular state of human society; because history,
that nourishes itself on revolutions, has taught the liberal man that there are revolutions that are necessary
and beneficial. As in the case of delayed births due to
fortuitous obstacles, where surgical operations are not
without danger and the belief that the birth is over-
due can be an error and the effect fatal, similarly un-
timely revolutions can initiate reaction, anarchy, and
barbarism. It is only natural that liberalism does not
approve of revolutionary turmoil, which, on its part,
except in extreme cases, it cautiously tries to avoid by
transforming, when possible, revolutions into evolu-
tions, and battles into negotiations and gradual
agreement.

The nineteenth century, during which liberty
reached its maximum awareness and greatest realization, found in *Faust,* which aspired to be not the divine but the human *Comedy* of the new era, the symbol of this ascension. For Faust, who searches for the
instant that he can order to a standstill once he feels
it to be the perfection of beauty, never finds that instant; and finally, when it seems that he has attained
it and *that word* comes to his lips, he discovers, not
the instant in which he may rest by extending it, but
an ideal that is superior to the instant and to material
pleasures: the restless operoseness in freedom.[3] This
is the reason why his soul does not fall prey to
Mephistopheles.

Liberalism is a secular and immanent conception;

while the communistic conception, for all its intrinsic materialism, gives birth to a sort of transcendence of the material principle. By this materialistic belief it enters into conflict with the Christian churches and also with the Catholic Church. Nevertheless, with the latter it has an incidental meeting ground in the suffocation that both impose upon the vigor of thought and action, and in the tendency to reduce human societies to the elementary level (to the level of children and men who are dedicated to the sole and therefore delusive chase after material goods). The Catholic Church can well accept these human societies, so spiritually exhausted, and can bend them to its power and dominion by pointing, as a reward for their miserable life on earth, to the heavenly beatitude.

However, the contrast between the liberal spirit and communism, with its impetuous simplifications and burning passions of resentment, hatred, and destruction, is profound. And one must be aware of this in order not to be subject to illusions of easy understanding and agreements; these things are certainly desirable but their accomplishment must of necessity be very laborious and slow. They require that one of the parties raise himself, by meditation and the lessons of experience, to a superior mental and cultural form whence, by looking at its previous concepts and plans, he will see them illumined and transformed, not more Utopian and unlimited, but limited and historical.

Now even when the communists or socialists believe themselves converted to the liberal conception, their culture, their affections, their spiritual needs, their knowledge, and historical penetration are completely different from and inferior to the liberal view of life;

and at the bottom of their souls there still persists the
ideal of a static society in which "social justice" may
be realized with the addition of "liberty," which in
them remains as an *epitheton ornans* (decorative epi-
thet). That is, they honor with words the concept of
liberty of which they have a completely superficial,
and not at all a profoundly dynamic, idea.

One finds confirmation of this in the recent example
of Henri De Man, whose book appeared in Italy a few
years ago: a book in which he announced his "surpas-
sing" of Marxism and his new belief in the liberal
faith or liberal-socialism. But some years of governmental life in his native Belgium have made him
aware that certain plans, which he believed to be
good, were obstructed and impeded in the parliament
by some vested interests or groups: personal interests
that seemed to him to prevail over the so-called, more
or less abstract "general interest." This has been sufficient to modify his views. Besides, the military defeat
of his people has been sufficient cause for him sol-
emnly to disavow the liberal system and pay his re-
spects to authoritarian and violent regimes as the only
ones that can assure the people the peace of inert material welfare and "social justice." [4]

Did Mr. De Man believe that whatever one of us,
in his particular world, holds to be true and useful
must not encounter obstacles and must be accepted
and realized by other men unhesitatingly? Does he believe that deceit and arrogance, and other wicked acts
that have always existed and that always will exist in
this world (acts that do not suppress the healthy and
progressive work of human society, as the whole record
of history testifies), need not exist? Does he believe

that, once the political structure is changed, reality, the *rugueuse réalité*, as Rimbaud called it in his only serious moment of interior crisis (and I am using this expression as my own because I like it), will become so smooth as to invite one's caressing hand? Rather, I fear that he sincerely believed in these strange things because *semel abbas semper abbas* (once an abbot, always an abbot). And he who does not have a spontaneous sense of history and of the drama and tragedy of human life never acquires, nor will ever acquire it, unless he sheds bloody sweat like that which moistened the earth in the Garden of Gethsemane.

Let us return to the history of communism and to its denial of history, which I have demonstrated above. What communism really denies, as I have already noted, is the autonomy or the positiveness of the subject, and not the framework of single positive acts which, under that word "communism," are well or badly classified—facts which, with their particular quality and for the influence they have exercised, certainly must enter into history.

In the most remote centuries, in the ancient world, in the Middle Ages, and in the first centuries of the modern era, the manifestations of communism were scarcely important, because they were the secondary manifestations of some religious crises, or episodic, savage explosions, or *jacqueries* of oppressed peasants. But in the course of the nineteenth century when true and proper socialistic parties and other similar institutions were formed, the encounter of socialistic forces with other historical forces operated, not primarily and directly, but certainly indirectly, toward the formation of so-called social legislation and made itself felt in other forms of legislation and administration and even today stimulates and causes daring reforms.

But the communist doctrine contributed also to the falsification and to the slander of the liberal system with captious interpretations and bitter satirical mottoes, by stupidly describing it as nothing but a series of conscious and even unconscious fictions and lies for the protection of the capitalist or bourgeois, and by insinuating doubt into the souls of many liberals themselves. Liberalism, therefore, began to lose its spiritual vigor and felt the loss of the self-confidence that had been the result of the awareness of its lofty, moral character. And the action of the socialistic parties aimed at the separation of the social classes, which they (the socialistic parties) claimed to represent, from the national or state entities to which they belonged: this, by repudiating the concept of country and every other concept of ethical content (European federation, society of nations, etc.) as capitalistic, bourgeois concepts.

Socialism spoke in the name of a nonexistent proletarian International, separated from the complexity and concreteness of historically specific interests; and finally, it espoused that unique revolutionary method, that the liberal system had eschewed in favor of the method of continuous struggle and of continuous, gradual, and legal progress, giving the revolutionary method only the function of a transitory expedient in exceptional cases. The anticipation of the revolution, converted to an ordinary or normal state of the soul, began to pave the way for what has taken place in many countries. But nowhere has establishment of the proletariat and communism been accomplished, except

in the destruction of liberal organizations and governments by authoritarian governments. The subject of
this history of the socialistic parties is not, however,
communism, but the *Christus patiens* (suffering
Christ), tormented and sorrowful humanity, which en-
dures its sorrowful trials yet does not succumb to them.

It would seem that the negative qualification that
we give to communism or to its history excludes the
particular socialistic or communistic conception called
Marxism: a conception that has effected, according to
Marx, the passage from Utopia to science; that inserts
itself into the historical course, as well as inaugurating
a new history in the realm of facts, with a corresponding historiographical autonomy in the realm of ideas.
But truly Marx did not live up to his formula, though
he and his friend Engels boasted about it a great deal.
The so-called insertion of communism into history was
not the bestowal upon the communist idea of a positive content which it lacked and continued to lack, but
simply one of the many witty dialectic inventions that
the Hegelian school, particularly the Left wing, used
to formulate.

Therefore, in that theoretical construction, the
course of history was seen as moving from an imaginary, primitive communism, and reaching its goal of a
reflexive and mature communism by passing through
the intermediary stages of the slave; servile and capitalistic economy; the ancient, medieval, and modern
economy; and finaly preparing to leap from the latter
to a so-called "Kingdom of Liberty."

Capitalistic dissolution, according to the criticism of
Marx, would result from the squanderings of wealth
caused by periodic crises. But at the same time he

could not help admiring the grandiose work done in a few decades by the industrious bourgeoisie, work that reduced to a somewhat secondary factor the economic losses caused by the crises of the economic order, and whose importance, extension, and periodic regularity Marx exaggerated. But Marx never clarified what he meant by that "Kingdom of Liberty," of which he spoke rhetorically. He said that capitalism was giving birth to and educating its own "gravediggers" in the working masses. But gravediggers are not, as we know, the creators of a new life, nor are they a destructive force that is also a constructive one. And the main point consists in specifying what is the new positive form that communism engenders on this earth.

Georges Sorel, who had more warmth of feeling and poetical impetus than Marx, dreamed of a proletarian class that would develop a more sincere and vibrant morality by again invigorating human society, as once Christianity had operated in the ancient world. Sorel took pleasure in comparing his cherished syndicalistic socialism with the Christian movement. But soon his dream faded; nor could he ever define or demonstrate the reality of the new morality, which was in its period of gestation and of which he was certainly neither a new Jesus nor a new Paul.

Marx limited himself to pointing out the future Promised Land in which, with classes abolished, there would be no more need of governmental apparatus and oppressions, because all individuals would enjoy absolute freedom of association. And when he was once asked to be a little more specific, he avoided the question with a joke: "I am not writing menus for the kitchens of the future." One unequivocal word came from his lips: "dictatorship"—a dictatorship to which he added the genitive, "of the proletariat"; but a dictatorship from which, whoever exercised it, one would not be able to see any escape.

Dictatorship, in the sense of a juridical institution, is that which is related to an established regime temporarily suspended and to which, once the exceptional conditions have been overcome, the intention is to return. But when this relationship is lacking (this relationship would be lacking in the case of the communist revolution which not only subverts the economy but also the idea of the state itself), dictatorship is not temporary but permanent and assumes another name with a different sound. Consequently, Marxian communism's only content is the lack of any—expressed in the absurd cessation of contrasts and in the historical void resulting from this cessation of the vital beat of life.

And in regard to the "actualization" that communism has in Russia nowadays, on another occasion and for the same purpose I have warned against the methodological error of pretending to solve a problem of principles by adducing a fact that cannot be assumed as a historical actuality; that is, thought, understood and defined only by means of principles that are themselves actually subject to doubt and discussion.

Thus we run in a vicious circle, that is the product of a lack of reflection. The nature and intrinsic contradictions and weakness of communism are one thing; what has happened and is happening in Russia is another. And only he who has investigated and meditated and understood the history of the Russian peo-

ple and society, of Russian thought, feeling, and customs, and what the Russian Revolution has built or
is building, can determine its character and make a
judgment.

On my part, I do not feel I am in possession of this
indispensable knowledge, and therefore I will not im-
provise a judgment on that history and society as many
persons do; I will not even assume the judgments of
others, though they seem to be authoritative, because
in order to accept another's judgment it is necessary
to be in a position to verify it with a critical eye and
therefore through a valid direct experience and
knowledge.

In English and American books I have come upon
reports from which one infers that among all the programs outlined by Marx only one has survived: dictatorship. This dictatorship does not derive from the
proletariat, but from a technical and political bureauc-
racy constituting a new class, rewarded more highly
than the ordinary citizenry, that cultivates its own
heirs by sending its children to universities and preparing their succession to governmental direction and
administration, while peasants and workers have no
freedom to transfer from one place to another and
are tied to the soil. Even the memory of Marx's dream
of the "Kingdom of Liberty" has been lost. And, concerning the "abolition of the state," there is silence by
tacit consent because, instead of abolition, there has
been an increase of state centralization: a centralization that regulates in its own way every task, every
thought. Even art and poetry have become political.

What is to be inferred from all this? That communism or the society of equals has not been established

in Russia? That communism, for intrinsic reasons, could not actualize itself has already been elucidated by criticism of its directive principle; and the fact that communism has not taken hold in Russia adds nothing to such an exposition. One cannot even say that the Russian Revolution confirms this exposition, because what has not yet happened could occur at another time and place, provided it is not logically contradictory and therefore impossible.

Thus one is again driven back to logical analysis. And the problem one must solve—it is a desperate one—is not the substitution of a fact, that has not been understood, for the elucidation of a principle necessary to understand the fact; the unique problem is the historically determinate fact—that is, how much that is new and progressive has Soviet Russia created in relation to czarist Russia? And since both are similarly autocratic, what is the quality of the new autocracy as compared to the old one?

One observes that if the old Russia did not make any philosophical contribution to the rest of Europe, it did, at least, give birth to poetic brilliance. The sorrowful and pessimistic poetry of Dostoevski and Tolstoy proceeded from souls who searched in vain for a path, while the new Russia does nothing but repeat some well-known Marxian formulas that were criticized and superseded half a century ago by the philosophy and economic science of Europe. Besides these formulas one also notices that because it is partisan and, as I have said, political, the poetry is usually inferior. But this negative consideration, because it is negative, is not historically conclusive, because artistic genius is born under every social condition. On the

other hand, materialistic thought, which is now cultivated in Russia and which is too weak to withstand
scholarly criticism, still can be relatively progressive;
that is, the beginning of progress and of elementary
scientific education in a people who have been deprived of these things and who, in their best minds,
have fed on semi-imaginary reasonings and paradoxes.
In spite of the lack of originality, of philosophical and
historical depth, and of high culture in modern Russia, progress is certainly to be found in the elementary
education abundantly provided for the Russian people—as was not done in the past—which has put an
end to the traditional analphabetism.

One still observes that, despite the preaching of
antipatriotic doctrines that follow the teachings of
Marx, who considered patriotism a middle-class feeling or fiction, and despite the internationalistic gospel
which reechoes the cry of the *Communist Manifesto*—
"Workers of the world, unite"—Russia feels itself to
be a nation among nations. It makes policies and alliances as a state among states, and not as one proletariat united with another against the capitalistic
structure. And it fights for the Russian fatherland.

The astonishment that prevails about this development is an effect of an erroneous presupposition: that
the subject of the new Russian history is communism.
It is really Russian life, which develops like that of
any other peoples and which, like that of any other
peoples, necessarily moves, if not in words, then in
actions, and through the same experiences, toward an
always greater or more apt, or less inept, freedom. One
must not forget that Russia has not separated itself, by
its revolution, from a regime that enjoyed liberty. Nor

has it fallen into a freedom more restricted than that of before. But, after a long incubation of ideas and spasmodic revolutionary attempts, it has made the only revolution—Russia was neither seventeenth-century England, nor the France of the eighteenth century, nor the Italy of the nineteenth century—of which it was capable, and which the best experts of its real conditions had already perceived within the forces at play.

And how the Russian people will develop in the future, only the future can say. It would be superfluous to speak here of the development we should like to see, because it has no relevance. And, in any case, our conception of development is implicit in our way of conceiving human life, its history, and its ideals.[5]

NOTES

Chapter 1

1. On this point see the sagacious essays of Giorgio Tagliacozzo, "Croce and the Nature of Economic Science," *The Quarterly Journal of Economics,* May 1945, Vol. LIX.

2. See Croce's *Conversazioni critiche* (Bari, 1951) V, 275.

3. In the 1875 Preface to the second edition of *Das Kapital.*

4. I refer to Röpke's *Gesellschaftskrisis der Gegenwart;* see Croce's *Discorsi di varia filosofia,* II, 194-99.

Chapter 2

1. Antonio Labriola (1843-1904), one of the most important Marxian thinkers of modern times, was the revered teacher of Croce. [Translator's note.]

Chapter 3

1. Carlo Marx, *Manoscritti economico-filosofici del 1844,* a cura di N. Bobbio (Einaudi: Torino, 1949).

Chapter 4

1. See the fourth edition prepared by Engels (Hamburg, 1890), I, XVII-XVIII.

2. See Antoni's essays on Marx: *Considerazioni su Hegel e Marx* (Ricciardi: Napoli, 1946), pp. 35-59.

3. This criticism of the *progressus ad finitum* as well as that of the *progressus ad infinitum,* and the demonstration of the concrete unity of both of them, were developed in my essay *Saggio sullo Hegel* (IV ediz.; Bari, 1948), pp. 144-71.

4. See the *Communist Manifesto.*

5. In regard to the substantial Hegelianism of Marx, and to the contradictions into which he falls by substituting Matter for the Idea, Gentile, then a Hegelian and a disciple of the Neapolitan Hegelians, gave a clear demonstration in his early book, *La filosofia di Marx.* In accepting now as then his demonstration of this historical-philosophical point of view, I wanted to treat another point of view not considered until now: that is, to demonstrate that the errors of Hegelian logic, which were not clarified by Marx, engendered the errors of his philosophical construction, historical and political, and remain ridiculously exaggerated in his modern mouthpieces.

Chapter 5

1. In the previous essay.

Chapter 5 (Continued)

2. See Engel's well-known book, on which Marx collaborated: *Dührings Umwälzung der Wissenschaft* (3. Aufl.; Stuttgart, 1894), pp. 274-86.

3. Since I do not have at hand the edition of Rjazanov, I quote from the small volume: Marx-Engels, *Über historischen Materialismus. Quellenbuch,* ed. H. Dunker (Berlin, 1930), pp. 71-72.

4. This essence is also to be found in the only Italian Marxist who seriously rethought and attempted to assimilate Marx: Antonio Labriola. See my *Materialismo storico ed economia marxistica* (VIII ediz.; Bari, 1945), pp. 305-6.

5. François Noel Babeuf (1760-1797) was a political agitator who was the first to propound socialism as a practical policy. [Translator's note.]

6. Louis Auguste Blanqui (1805-1881) was a French socialist who was the first public advocate of the dictatorship of the proletariat. [Translator's note.]

7. The thought, developed later by Engels in his writings on Feuerbach, is already in the Marxian *Critica della filosofia di Hegel,* which bears the date 1844.

8. *Über historischen Materialismus, op. cit.,* p. 72.

9. O. Maenchen-Helfen and B. Nicolajevsk, *Karl Marx* (Gallimard: Paris, 1937).

10. Croce, *Materialismo storico ed economia marxistica, op. cit.,* pp. 109-11 *n.*

Chapter 5 (Continued)

11. Marx himself felt the moral acridity of his style but he could not erase it because, though he was unaware of the reason, it was inherent in his research, not essentially scientific, that produced *Das Kapital* and that distorted the economic meaning of "value."

12. Anselm (1033-1109) is a well-known thinker for his a priori argument for God's existence. God is a being greater than any conceivable being. Therefore, this being, which is such that no greater can be conceived, exists, without any doubt, both in mind and in reality. [Translator's note.]

13. "Lettres sur la philosophie de l'histoire": in *Oeuvres choisies* de Pierre Tschadaïeff, publiées pour la première fois par le P. Gagarin de la Compagnie de Jésus (Frank: Paris-Leipzig, 1862), pp. 23, 26, 27.

Chapter 6

1. See Croce, *Etica e politica* (IV ediz.; Bari, 1956), pp. 321-28.

Chapter 7

1. Werner Sombart, *Der Bourgeois, Zur Geistesgeschichte der modernen Wirtschaftsmenschen* (1913).

2. Bernhard Groethuisen, *Die Enstehung der bürgerlichen Welt und Lebensanschauung in Frankreich* (Niemeyer: Halle a.S., 1927).

Chapter 8

1. Angelo A. De Gennaro, *The Philosophy of Bene-detto Croce* (The Citadel Press: New York, 1961), pp. 34-42. [Translator's note.]

2. Vittorio Alfieri (1749-1803), the greatest tragic dramatist of Italy, was an early exponent of the concept of Italian political unity based on inde-pendence and liberty. [Translators note.]

Chapter 10

1. Carlo Pisacane (1818-1857) was one of the heroes of the Italian Risorgimento. In 1857, he fitted out an expedition which set out from Genoa and landed at Sapri, in Calabria, in order to arouse the people against the Bourbon government; but the local police, assisted by the peasantry, attacked the band and, among others, killed Pisacane. [Translator's note.]

2. The *City of the Sun* is a book written by the Ital-ian philosopher Tommaso Campanella (1568-1639) where he, under Platonic inspiration, sketches an ideal state based on communism of wives and goods, and ruled by philosopher-priests. [Translator's note.]

3. See Croce, *Filosofia e storiografia* (Bari, 1949), pp. 122-27.

4. See the essay "Considerazioni sul problema morale dei nostri giorni" in Croce's *Pensiero politico e politica attuale* (Bari, 1946), pp. 3-24.

Chapter 11

1. *Geschichte des Sozialismus in Einzeln-Darstellungen* (Dietz: Stuttgart, 1895).

2. Croce, *Materialismo storico ed economia marxistica* (IX ediz.; Bari, 1951), pp. 188-89.

3. The idea of freedom is expressed in the very famous verses by Goethe which are always worthy of meditation:

   Des ist der Weisheit letzter Schluss
   Nur der verdient sich Freiheit wie das Leben,
   Der täglich sie erobern muss.
   Und so verbringt, umrungen von Gefahr,
   Hier Kindheit, Mann und Greis sein tüchtig Jahr.
   Solch ein Gewimmel möcht' ich sehn,
   Auf freiem Grund mit freiem Volke stehen.
   Zum Augenblicke dürft' ich sagen:
   Verweile doch, du bist so schön!

   (The last result of wisdom stamps it true:
   He only earns his freedom and existence,
   Who daily conquers them anew.
   Thus here, by dangers girt, shall glide away
   Of childhood, manhood, age, the vigorous day:
   And such a throng I fain would see,—
   Stand on free soil among a people free!
   Then dared I hail the Moment fleeing:
   "Ah, still delay—thou art so fair!")

   Translated by Bayard Taylor

4. Henri De Man, *Après coup, mémoires* (édit. de la maison d'or; Bruxelles, 1941).

5. See the end of my *Storia d'Europa nel secolo decimonono,* published in 1932.

SOURCES

CHAPTER 1

Filosofia e storiografia (Bari, 1949), pp. 224-30.

CHAPTER 2

Ibid., pp. 289-94.

CHAPTER 3

Indagini su Hegel (Bari, 1952), pp. 98-103.

CHAPTER 4

Filosofia e storiografia, op. cit., pp. 259-69.

CHAPTER 5

Ibid., pp. 270-80.

CHAPTER 6

Discorsi di varia filosofia (Bari, 1959), II, pp. 188-94.

CHAPTER 7

Etica e politica (IV ediz.; Bari, 1956), pp. 328-37.

CHAPTER 8

Filosofia e storiografia, op. cit., pp. 231-38.

CHAPTER 9

Conversazioni critiche (Bari, 1951), V, pp. 207-15.

CHAPTER 10

Indagini su Hegel, op. cit., pp. 104-20.

CHAPTER 11

Discorsi di varia filosofia, op. cit., I, pp. 277-90.

SELECTED BIBLIOGRAPHY

I Works of Croce

Materialismo storico ed economia marxistica, 1900.
Estetica come scienza dell'espressione e linguistica generale, 1902.
Logica come scienza del concetto puro, 1909.
Filosofia della pratica, 1909.
Teoria e storia della storiografia, 1917.
Conversazioni critiche (1918 ff.) (5 volumes).
Saggio sullo Hegel, 1907.
Problemi di estetica, 1910.
La filosofia di Giambattista Vico, 1911.
Breviario di estetica, 1913.
Cultura e vita morale, 1914.
Ariosto, 1917.
Contributo alla critica di me stesso, 1918.
Primi saggi, 1919.
Pagine sparse, 1919.
Goethe, 1919.
La poesia di Dante, 1920.
Nuovi saggi di estetica, 1920.
Frammenti di etica, 1922.
Elementi di politica, 1925.
Storia d'Europa nel secolo decimonono, 1932.
Storia d'Italia dal 1871 al 1915, 1927.
Storia dell' età barocca in Italia, 1929.
Ultimi saggi, 1935.

La poesia, 1936.
La storia come pensiero e come azione, 1938.
Il carattere della filosofia moderna, 1941.
Discorsi di varia filosofia (1945 ff.) (2 volumes).
Filosofia e storiografia, 1949.
Indagini su Hegel, 1952.

ALL THESE BOOKS WERE PUBLISHED BY
LATERZA INC., BARI.

II Books About Croce

LUIGI RUSSO, La critica letteraria contemporanea in Italia (Laterza: Bari, 1942), Vol. I.
G. CASTELLANO, Benedetto Croce (Laterza: Bari, 1936).
CARLO ANTONI, Commento A Croce (Pozza: Venice, 1955).
ANGELO A. DE GENNARO, The Philosophy of Benedetto Croce (The Citadel Press: New York, 1961).
GIAN N. ORSINI, Benedetto Croce (Southern Illinois Press: Carbondale, Ill., 1961).
A. ROBERT CAPONIGRI, History and Liberty; The Historical Writings of Benedetto Croce (Routledge and Paul: London, 1955).

III Articles About Croce

HAYDEN V. WHITE, "The Abiding Relevance of Croce's Idea of History," The Journal of Modern History, Vol. XXXV (1963), pp. 104-24.

R. T. THOLFSEN, "What is Living in Croce's 'Theory of History,'" *The Historian,* Vol. XXIII (1961), pp. 283-302.

ANGELO A. DE GENNARO, "Storia e Storicismo," *Italica,* Vol. XXX, (1953), pp. 231-237.

ANGELO A. DE GENNARO, "Croce and Vico," *The Journal of Aesthetics and Art Criticism,* Vol. XXII (1963), pp. 43-7.

ANGELO A. DE GENNARO, "An Approach to Benedetto Croce," *The Personalist,* Vol. XLII, (1961), pp. 21-7.

M. E. BROWN, "Croce's Early Aesthetics," *The Journal of Aesthetics and Art Criticism,* Vol. XXII (1963), pp. 29-41.